First published 1972
Macdonald and Co
(Publishers) Limited
St Giles House
49-50 Poland Street
London W1

Made and printed by
Morrison and Gibb Limited
Edinburgh, Scotland

Editor
Angela Littler

Illustrators
Malcolm McGregor
Patricia Lenander
John Yates
Peter Harverson

Production
Stephen Pawley
Philip Hughes

Picture Research
Penny Warn
Jackie Newton

Sources of Photographs
Graham Pizzey/Bruce Coleman Ltd.
Harald Schultz/Bruce Coleman Ltd.
Jane Burton/Bruce Coleman Ltd.
David Hughes/Bruce Coleman Ltd.
Imperial Chemical Industries Ltd.
Mrs. J. L. B. Smith
Dr. Maurice Burton

Series devised by
Peter Usborne

ISBN 0 356 04096 8
Library of Congress Catalog Card
No. 72-88053

The Life of
Fishes

A simple introduction to the way fishes live and behave for younger readers. Special reference and projects section

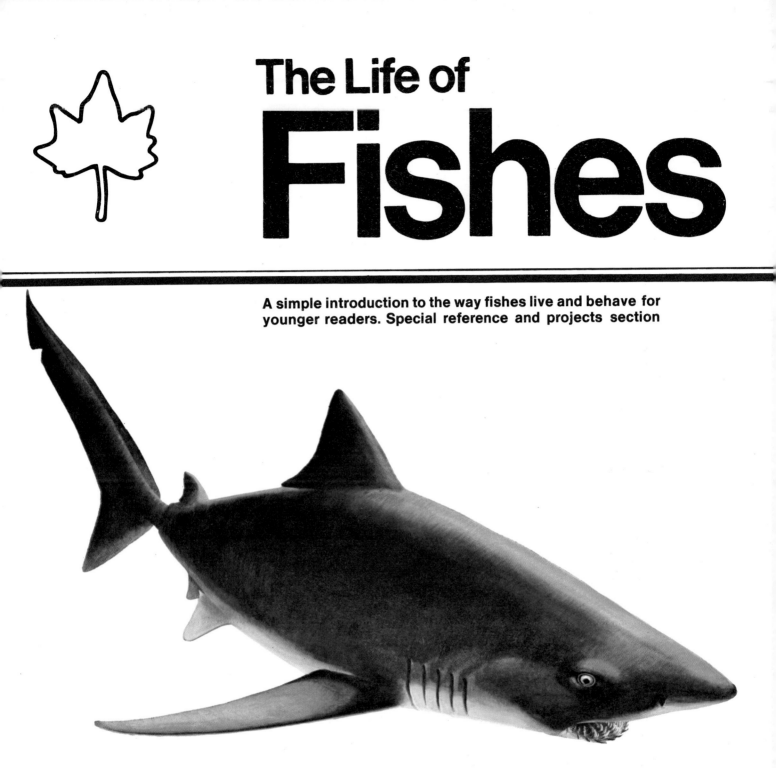

Macdonald
Educational

LONDON · NEW YORK · TORONTO

Dr. Maurice Burton

The Life of Fishes

For a long time there were many mysteries about how deep-sea fishes live, how they find their food, and find each other at mating time, and what the purpose of their light-organs was. There was the mystery of where and how eels breed, and how the salmon finds its way back to the river in which it was born. Not all these mysteries have been solved, but much more is known today than even ten years ago. Fifty years ago, very little was known about the sounds fishes make. Then, during the Second World War, as a result of submarine warfare, a whole programme of research into fish noises was begun.

These and other new discoveries are found in this book, together with information about the everyday things fishes do.

Fishes, unlike birds and many mammals, inhabit what is to man a hostile environment. *The Life of Fishes* explores this environment, and traces the evolution of under-water life. It shows the amazing variety of colour, shape and size of fishes, explains how they feed, and describes the brilliant camouflage of many fishes. It looks at their scales, spines and armour, their defence mechanisms, colour changes, and the long, instinctive migrations that many fishes make.

The book ends with a reference and projects section packed with more information and practical suggestions to follow.

Contents

The First Fishes	8
Records of the Past	10
The Shallow Seas	12
River Fishes	13
Moving through Water	14
Breathing Underwater	16
Colour and Colour Change	18
Camouflage for Safety	20
Inside a Fish	22
The Food Chain	24
Courting and Nesting	26
How are Fishes Born?	28
Growing Up	30
Scales and Spines	31
Journey of a Lifetime	32
Fishes of the Deeps	34
Tropical Fishes	36
Poison and Electricity	38
Flying and Talking	39
Friends and Enemies	40
Strange Fishes	42
Man and the Sea	44
Pollution	46
Myths and Legends	48

Reference and Projects

Facts and Figures	49
Distribution of Fishes	52
Keeping Goldfish	54
Checking Pollution	56
How to Draw Fishes	58
Names and Orders	59
Index to Pictures and Text	60

The First Fishes

All life began in the sea. Fishes developed in the water. Most of them never left it. Others learnt to live on dry land.

Jamoytius, about nine inches long. A very early fossil, over 400 million years old. Shows what first vertebrate may have looked like.

Cephalaspis (kef-a-las-pis), about nine inches long. Armoured, jawless fish which sucked in its food. Lived in rivers 350–400 million years ago.

Osteolepis, about twelve inches long. Lived nearly 400 million years ago. It was a true fish. Fishes like Osteolepis first came out on land to live.

Xenacanthus, about nine inches long. One of the first sharks. Lived 350 million years ago.

Some fishes crawled out of the water onto dry land. They stayed longer and longer. Their fins gradually became legs and they lost their gills. Some became frogs and toads. Others changed into reptiles, the ancestors of birds and mammals.

The Beginning
Life began in the sea, many millions of years ago, before man appeared. The first living things were microscopic plants. This is the way scientists today describe things that are so small they can only be seen under a microscope. Some of these plants began to eat the others. They were the first animals. Gradually, some of the plants and animals grew bigger. Some animals became sea anemones, jellyfishes, worms, starfishes, snails or crabs.

The Fishes
A few of the sea animals grew a backbone, and became the first fishes. They grew fins, and breathed with gills. Some of them had lungs as well. Some fishes dragged themselves onto dry land. Very slowly, they evolved, or adapted, in different ways to the change in their surroundings.

Two Types of Fishes
There are now two main kinds of fishes. The sharks have a skeleton of gristle, or cartilage, and live mainly in the sea. The bony, or true fishes have skeletons of bone. Many live in rivers or lakes. Some other fishes, like lampreys and hagfishes, have no jaws, and are descended from fishes like Cephalaspis above.

Today, there are about 30,000 different kinds of fishes.

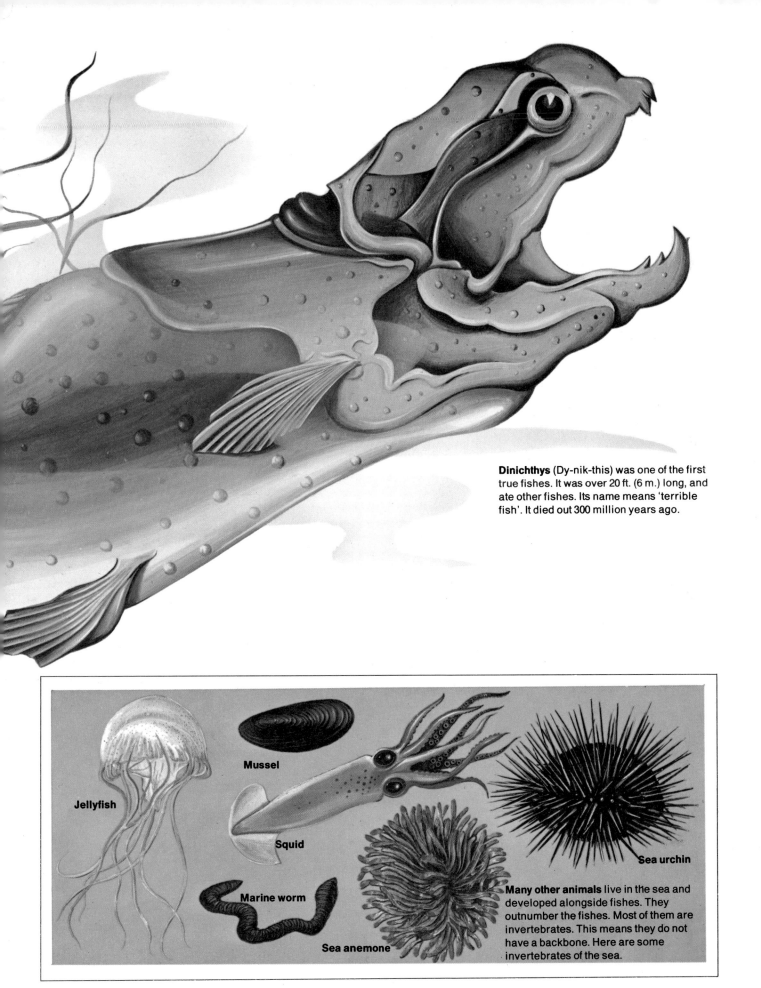

Dinichthys (Dy-nik-this) was one of the first true fishes. It was over 20 ft. (6 m.) long, and ate other fishes. Its name means 'terrible fish'. It died out 300 million years ago.

Jellyfish

Mussel

Squid

Marine worm

Sea anemone

Sea urchin

Many other animals live in the sea and developed alongside fishes. They outnumber the fishes. Most of them are invertebrates. This means they do not have a backbone. Here are some invertebrates of the sea.

9

Records of the Past

Fossils are a permanent record of what animals were like years ago. Fossils are often millions of years old.

A dead fish is washed up on the shore. It lies between the high and low tide lines. This fish may become a fossil.

The bones of the fish are picked clean by seabirds looking for food. Soon it is just a skeleton.

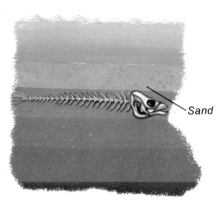

The skeleton gradually gets buried in the sand. It will slowly become flattened out by the weight above it.

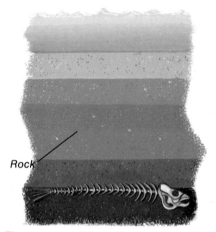

The pressure of the earth above turns the layer of sand to rock.

Sometimes, especially in early history, earthquakes and upheavals changed the shape of the land. Here, the land has risen above the sea.

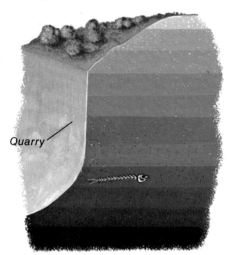

Later, men have dug a quarry into the side of the hill. They want the slate or chalk which they can find there.

A paleontologist—a man who studies fossils —thinks that the quarry is a likely place to look for fossils. He digs with a pick at the side of the quarry.

The paleontologist has found a stone which may contain a fossil. He breaks it open. It will split cleanly in two.

The stone has split, to show a perfect fossil. All that remains of the fish above is the shape of its bones preserved for so long.

Fossils

The name 'fossil' comes from a Latin word meaning to dig up. Fossils are dug out of the ground. They may be in soft earth or they may have to be chipped out of hard rock. Some are hundreds of millions of years old. Others may only be a million or less.

When an Animal Dies

Animals are dying all the time. Some are eaten by scavenging animals. Some animals may be only partly eaten or not eaten at all. They are just buried. In the sea, dead animals are buried by silt brought down by rivers. In rivers, animals get buried by mud. On land, dead leaves cover them. These leaves decay and later turn to earth.

Some dead bodies get buried quickly, others slowly. The more quickly they get buried, the more perfect are their fossils. Only one out of tens or hundreds of thousands of animals that die becomes a fossil.

As time goes on, more silt, mud or earth collects over them. They sink farther and farther into the ground. The load of silt, mud or earth over them presses hard and rock is formed with the fossil inside.

Movements in the earth's crust bring deeply buried fossils near the surface. So fossils may be found on mountains and hillsides, in quarries and chalk pits, or deep in the ground, in coal mines, for example.

Why are Fossils Important?

Fossils are important because they show what animals were like years ago. They also show which animals have become extinct. Usually only the hard parts, the skeletons, are fossilized. In some fossils, however, even the soft parts, such as the stomach, are preserved. Some fossils of fishes are so well preserved that even the colours of the skin can be seen quite clearly.

Animals living in or over water are the most likely to be fossilized. They get buried quickly by silt or mud. That is why there are so many fossils of fishes. Birds and bats stand the least chance of being made into fossils. That is why so little is known of their past history.

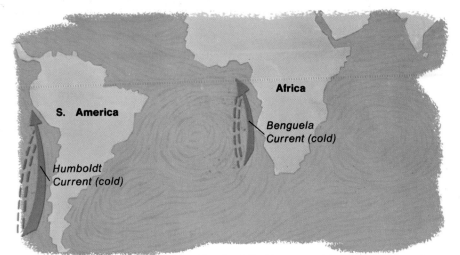

In many parts of the world there are cold and hot currents. Currents are like rivers running through the sea. If these currents shift one way or the other, thousands of fishes may be killed because of the sudden change in temperature. When thousands of fishes die at once this is called a mass death.

When a mass death of fishes happens, many are washed ashore. Another cause of mass death is a sudden 'bloom' of plant plankton, the microscopic plants of the sea. A quick growth of plankton turns the sea red and is poisonous for the fishes. These blooms are called red tides.

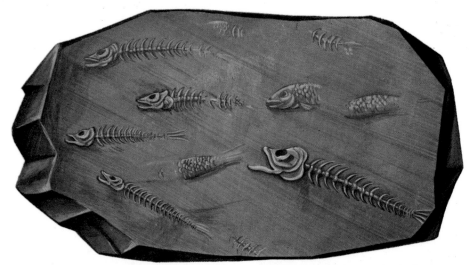

Mass deaths have happened at other times in the world's history. Sometimes, large slabs of rock are found, filled with fossil fish skeletons. They look just like the scenes on beaches today when mass deaths happen. The fishes in a mass death are usually all of one kind. They are not a mixture of species.

11

The Shallow Seas

The shallow seas lie beyond the low tide mark, and before the ocean. Many kinds of fishes live there.

What are the Shallow Seas?

The seas can be divided roughly into three types. There is the part which borders on the edge of continents and islands, where the sea ebbs and flows with each tide. This is the sea-shore, called 'the littoral' by scientists. Beyond the low tide mark are the shallow seas, which go down to depths of 600 feet (about 180 metres). Their average depth, however, is about 200 feet (60 metres). Beyond that is the ocean.

Two-thirds of the earth's surface is covered with salt water. If all the salt were dried out of the sea and spread evenly over the earth it would make a continuous layer 200 feet (60 metres) deep.

Fishes of the Shallow Seas

Some fishes move from the shallow seas to the surface waters of the ocean, like the fishes in the top right-hand corner of the picture above. The flying fishes are mainly oceanic, but do sometimes come nearer the coasts. Tuna fishes make long migrations so are sometimes in the open sea, sometimes in the shallow seas. The same can be said for the large ocean sunfish.

The rest of the fishes shown above are more or less permanent residents in the shallow seas. Some, like the puffer fishes and porcupine fishes, belong to the warm seas. Mackerel and herring belong to the cooler seas of the temperate region.

Parrot fishes and surgeon fishes are found especially round the coral reefs of the warm seas.

Habitat

About two-thirds of the 30,000 different kinds of fishes live in the sea. Sea fishes are more varied than river and lake fishes, because the habitats of the sea all differ greatly. A habitat is the place in which an animal lives. In the seas there can be rocky habitats, sandy and muddy habitats, coral reefs, kelp (seaweed) beds, as well as surf beaches, calm bays, shallow seas and deep seas. The sea is the environment, or surroundings, where all these habitats are found.

River Fishes

Many fishes do not live in the sea. They spend all or most of their lives in rivers. They are not as varied as sea fishes.

Frog

Mallard

300 mm.

Salmon

Minnow

Dace

Trout

600 mm.

Perch

Roach

900 mm.

Pike

Gudgeon

Carp

1.2 m.

1.5 m.

Bullhead

Stone loach

Eel

Where do Rivers Come From?

Rivers start as springs. Water from rain and melting snow collects under the ground. Then it flows out at one spot, called a spring. The water cuts a groove, or bed, in the ground. The bed gets broader and broader on its way to the sea.

When a river runs over level ground it flows slowly. When flowing from high ground it runs swiftly. Apart from this, all rivers are much alike. There are not as many different habitats in rivers as there are in the sea. So river fishes are all much alike.

The difference between the seas and the rivers is like the difference between a large factory and a small factory. The large factory can produce many more kinds of goods than the small factory, because it can have many kinds of workshops.

Eels

Eels are unusual because they live in fresh water but breed in the sea. Eels are really marine fishes that have come into rivers and lakes to live, but go back to the sea to breed.

Food

Some river fishes feed on plant food, scraping small plants from rocks and stones with their teeth. Others take small animals such as worms from the mud on the bottom. Most of the fishes feed on freshwater shrimps, water fleas and insects, either the larvae or the adult insects that fall into the water. A few eat smaller fishes.

Fast and Slow

In a fast-flowing river, there are usually fewer fishes than in a slower river, because it is not a good environment. Fast-moving water sweeps along anything in its path. It sweeps away plants, and would sweep away fishes, too. However, those fishes that can be found in a fast-moving river are often a flattish shape, and are adapted for clinging or holding onto rocks and boulders. They cannot be swept away even by a torrential stream.

Moving through Water

Fishes are adapted to glide smoothly through water. Most of them have a streamlined shape.

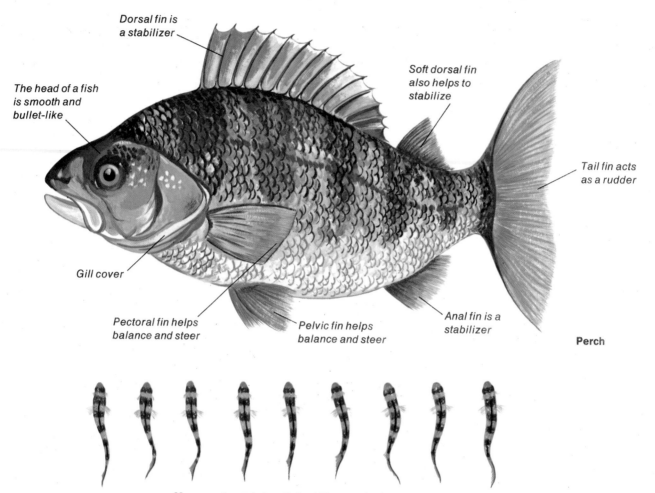

Dorsal fin is a stabilizer

The head of a fish is smooth and bullet-like

Soft dorsal fin also helps to stabilize

Tail fin acts as a rudder

Gill cover

Pectoral fin helps balance and steer

Pelvic fin helps balance and steer

Anal fin is a stabilizer

Perch

Movements made by a fish making one body stroke

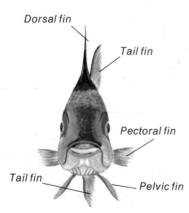

Dorsal fin

Tail fin

Pectoral fin

Tail fin

Pelvic fin

A fish has a streamlined shape. This means that it has a smooth surface, with no lumps on the body. It can move through the water easily. Notice how smooth the surface of a fish's head is. It offers no resistance to the flow of water around it.

Moving in Water

It is harder for people to move through water than through air. Water is thicker. Although it is quite easy to swim through water, it is very difficult to walk upright. Men made boats to move over the water. The first boats were round, almost like big saucers. They were slow and rowing them was hard work. Then someone hit upon the idea of making the boat pointed in front, like all boats are today. When the first submarine was made it was like a barrel. It was not a success. Then a submarine was made that was long and pointed at each end. This travelled faster under water. Without knowing it, the men who made it were copying the shape of a fish.

The cigar-shape is best for letting water flow past, so allowing the fish—or the submarine—to slide through the water. All fishes except ones like trunkfishes and sea-horses swim by waggling the body and the tail. The movement is like that of a snake or serpent on land. So it is called a serpentine movement. As a snake moves over the ground different parts of its body press in turn against the little bumps in the surface of the ground, pushing the body forward. When a fish wriggles its body it presses against the water and drives itself forward.

14

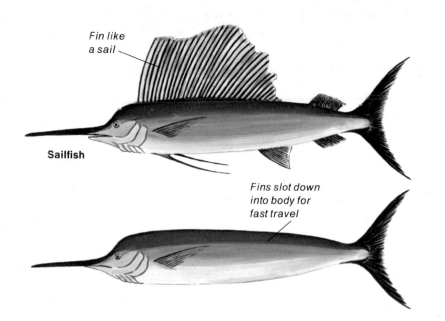

Fin like a sail

Sailfish

Fins slot down into body for fast travel

Water flows easily over the rounded stones in a shallow stream. A log with stumps of branches on it makes the water boil and bubble round it. This is because the bumpy shape of the log is holding up the flow of the water. A smooth object allows the water to flow easily round it. A cigar-shaped fish with a smooth surface slides easily through the water.

The sailfish lives in warm seas. It has a large fin on its back, which looks like a sail when it is raised. It has other fins as well which act as balancers, to keep it the right way up in the water. When the sailfish wants to move quickly it folds the sail into a groove running along the middle of its back. The other fins, except for the tail fin, drop into grooves in the body. The jaws of the sailfish are long and pointed, and can cut easily through the water. So with all fins stowed away a sailfish can shoot through the water at 60 m.p.h. (96.5 k.p.h.).

Strange Swimmers

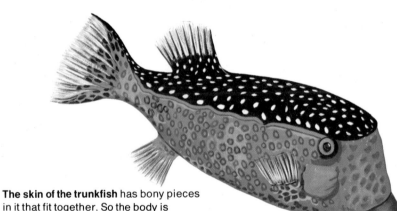

The skin of the trunkfish has bony pieces in it that fit together. So the body is enclosed in a box, or trunk. The trunkfish can only swim slowly and it cannot waggle its body to swim. It has to scull with its fins.

Shrimpfishes hide, often upside down, among the spines of a sea urchin. The black lines on the sides of their bodies look like the spines of the sea urchin. They are hidden from enemies.

The body of the seahorse is covered in bony armour. It swims upright. It does not waggle its body to swim. It gently waves the little fin on its back, which acts as a propellor, pushing the fish along.

Catfishes are so called because they have long whiskers around their mouths. There are catfishes in Africa that always swim upside down. Nobody can say why they do this.

Ordinary fishes have a coloured back and a white belly (see page 18). Upside-down catfishes often have a dark belly, because this is the side which is upper-most, and needs dark camouflage.

Breathing Underwater

Both fishes and men need oxygen to breathe. Men get it from the air. Fishes get it from the water.

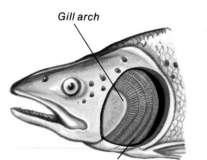

Gill arch

Under each gill cover are several rows of gill filaments. The water passes over these and oxygen is taken out.

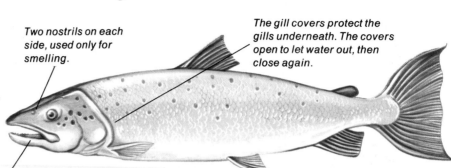

Two nostrils on each side, used only for smelling.

The gill covers protect the gills underneath. The covers open to let water out, then close again.

The mouth opens and closes to swallow water.

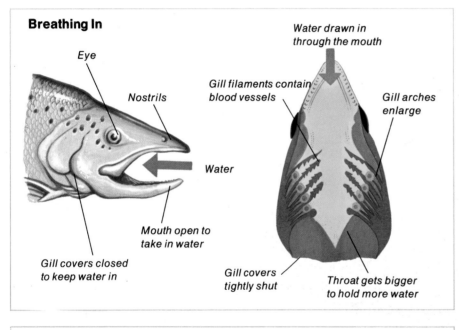

Breathing In

Eye

Nostrils

Water

Mouth open to take in water

Gill covers closed to keep water in

Water drawn in through the mouth

Gill filaments contain blood vessels

Gill arches enlarge

Gill covers tightly shut

Throat gets bigger to hold more water

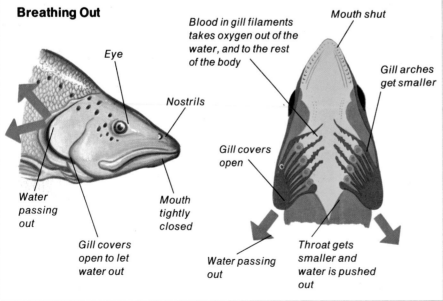

Breathing Out

Eye

Nostrils

Water passing out

Mouth tightly closed

Gill covers open to let water out

Blood in gill filaments takes oxygen out of the water, and to the rest of the body

Mouth shut

Gill arches get smaller

Gill covers open

Water passing out

Throat gets smaller and water is pushed out

Gills

A fish breathes by gills. The gills are on either side of the head, and each set is usually covered outside by a gill cover. To breathe, a fish gulps water through its mouth into its throat.

On each side of the throat are slits leading into the gill chamber. The throat between the slits is supported by gill arches. These are arches of bone in the bony fishes, and cartilage in sharks and rays. Each gill arch has a double row of gill filaments. These are red, because they contain a fine network of blood vessels.

Oxygen is removed from the water here and taken to the rest of the body in the blood. Oxygen is needed to keep the life processes going.

The gill filaments not only help take in oxygen, they also give out waste matter like that which is usually strained out of the blood by the kidneys. The filaments also pass carbon dioxide from the blood. This is a gas which is given off when oxygen is used up in keeping the life processes going. It is therefore another waste substance.

Gill Rakers

On the inside of each gill arch is a double row of what look like soft bristles, pointing inwards into the throat. They are the gill rakers. They are short in most fishes. In

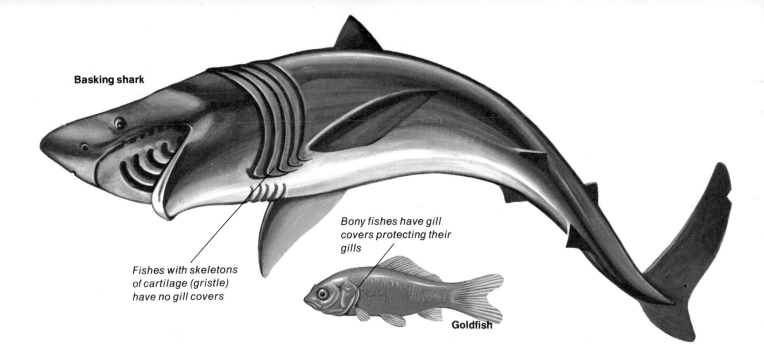

Basking shark

Fishes with skeletons of cartilage (gristle) have no gill covers

Bony fishes have gill covers protecting their gills

Goldfish

plankton-feeders the front row interlocks with the hind row in a trellis. This acts as a sieve, stopping any small particles taken in with the water. This is so that the gills do not get clogged. In fishes that feed on tiny plankton, the plankton is sieved by the gill rakers. Then it passes down the throat to the stomach to be digested.

Nostrils

In most fishes, nostrils are used only for smelling, not for breathing. The nostrils each have a way in and a way out. Water goes in through one nostril, passes over the smelling organ, and then goes out through the other nostril.

Gill Covers

The gills of both bony and cartilaginous fishes are the same except for one thing. In bony fishes the gill chamber is covered by a lid. In sharks and rays (cartilaginous fishes) the gills have no cover. So they are called naked gills. A bony fish can close its gill chamber, by pulling down the lid. So it can control its breathing. In this way it can 'hold its breath' or it can breathe more quickly, depending on whether it is resting, swimming slowly, or swimming fast. A shark cannot rest. It must keep swimming all the time so that there is always a flow of water across the gill filaments to enable it to breathe.

Breathing Out of Water

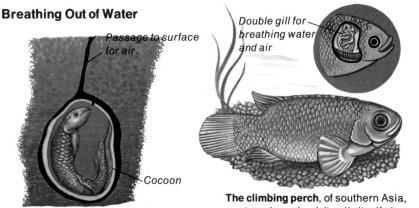

Passage to surface for air

Cocoon

Double gill for breathing water and air

Lungfishes live in the Tropics. They have lungs as well as gills. They can go to sleep when the rivers dry up in the hot weather. This is the opposite of hibernating. It is called aestivating. The fish makes a cocoon in the mud, with a hole to the surface for air to get in.

The climbing perch, of southern Asia, can travel overland. It pulls itself along by the edges of its gill covers. It has a double gill. One part breathes water, the other breathes air.

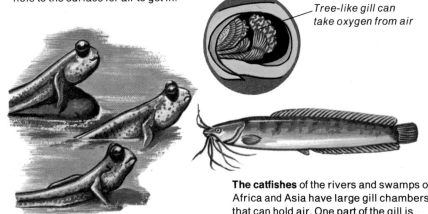

Tree-like gill can take oxygen from air

The little mudskippers of the Tropics leave the sea at low tide and skip over the mud feeding on sandhoppers. Mudskippers carry a supply of water in the gills. They must go back to a pool from time to time to renew the water.

The catfishes of the rivers and swamps of Africa and Asia have large gill chambers that can hold air. One part of the gill is tree-like. It can take oxygen from the air, so catfishes can live in foul water. They also come on land at night to catch insects. They carry with them a supply of air in the gill chamber. This enables them to breathe out of water.

Colour and Colour Change

The colours of a fish are useful as well as attractive. Some fishes can change their colours to match their surroundings.

Markings

Zebra fishes have dark lines on their bodies. The lines give a false impression of speed. An enemy may miss its mark when it tries to snap up a fish.

Angelfishes move very slowly among weeds. The dark lines on their body look like upright stems of weeds.

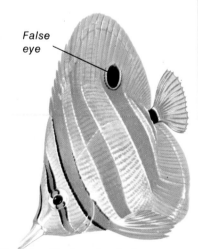

False eye

There is a black spot on the long-nosed butterfly fish, and its enemies cannot tell whether it is coming or going.

Most fishes are darker on the back than on the underside. When an enemy looks up at a fish the silvery belly tones in with the sky. To an enemy looking down on a fish the dark back makes it hard to see against the bottom of the river, like this trout among stones.

Fishes living in the sea or in rivers have a dark back and a silvery belly. A sea fish's body is also sometimes iridescent, or mirror-like, as well. The silver of the belly is caused by crystals in the skin reflecting light, like a mirror. They are called iridocytes. Sometimes they break up the light and scatter it, giving several colours.

Colour

All fishes are coloured in a special way. They are usually dark on top, and lighter underneath. This is so that if an enemy looks down from above, the fish blends in with the dark water. An enemy looking up from below cannot see the lighter underside of the fish against the light from the surface. River fishes are usually a brownish colour on top, and sea fishes are more silvery.

Change

Some fishes can change their colours according to their backgrounds. This is especially true of flatfishes that lie on the sea bed, and cannot swim very fast. It is a form of pro-tection against their enemies. Some flatfishes can adapt to almost any background.

How is it Done?

If a flatfish is put with its head on a dark background, and the rest of its body on a light background, it will soon turn the darker colour. It seems, therefore, that the fish uses sight when it changes colour.

Many fishes cannot change col-our, but have lines or bars across their bodies which break up their outline against the water. This makes them difficult to see. Some, like the butterfly fish, have false eyes which deceive enemies.

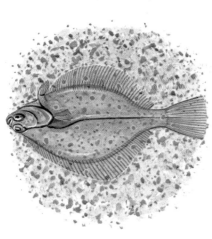

Flatfishes, such as plaice, can change colour to copy the background on which they are lying. On gravel they gradually turn mottled to match the stones.

Flatfishes can change colour to suit almost any background, even a chessboard. But they do so less easily on an artificial background.

* **Black chromatophore**

* **Yellow chromatophore**

* **Iridocyte**

Chromatophores (kro-mat-o-fors) are tiny bags of pigment in the skin. Each chromatophore contains several primary colours, like grains of coloured powder used for mixing poster colours. When the bag contracts and the grains are all bunched together the fish looks pale or white. As the bag expands the coloured grains spread out. The iridocytes give a mirror-like shine to the skin.

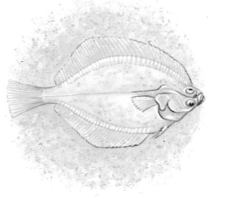

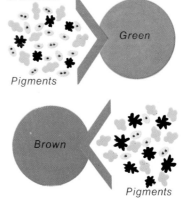

Pigments → *Green*

Brown ← *Pigments*

A flounder lying on dark mud soon begins to change colour over its upper surface. After a while it seems to disappear, because it has taken on the colour of the mud.

Flounders can also change to a light colour. So they become sand coloured after lying on sand for a few minutes. They are very hard to see against the background.

Bright Colours

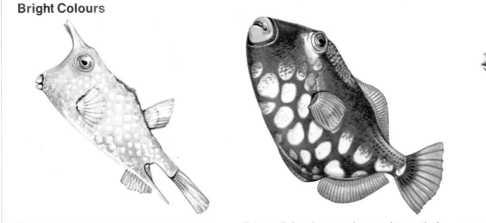

Trunkfishes give out a poison from their skin when they are touched. This can kill small fishes. Their bright colours warn others to leave them alone.

Triggerfishes have a sharp spine on their backs. Their bright colours may be to warn other fishes to leave them alone.

The brightly coloured cuckoo wrasse is good to eat. It changes to even brighter colours when it is courting.

Camouflage for Safety

Camouflage is useful to keep a fish hidden, either from its enemies or from its prey.

The leaffish of South America is brown. When danger is near it floats, so that it looks like a dead leaf. There is a short stump on its snout that looks like a leaf stalk.

The carpet shark of Australia is also called the wobbegong. It is more flattened, and lies on the bottom more than most sharks. Its skin has got a pattern rather like the pattern on a carpet. This helps to disguise it on the sea bed.

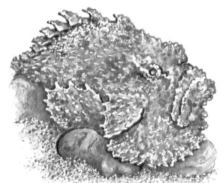

The stonefish of Australia lies perfectly still among stones and seaweed. It looks exactly like them. On its back it has sharp spines sticking up. These give out a very powerful poison when the spines are touched.

Seaweed

The sea dragon lives in the waters around Australia. It is about six inches (152 mm.) long. It has ragged flaps of skin hanging from different parts of its body. It looks like a piece of floating seaweed.

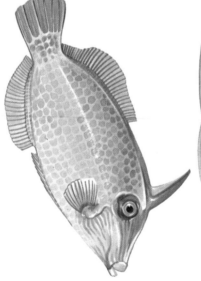

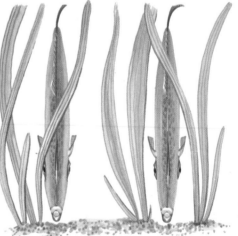

File fishes of tropical seas are coloured like seaweeds. They also rest head downwards on the sea bottom, among seaweed. They sway gently, and look just like seaweed waving in the current.

The Hunter and the Hunted

Most animals use camouflage. This means they are coloured like their natural surroundings. They also try by their behaviour to keep hidden. The only exceptions are animals that carry poison or a sting, or are in some other way unpleasant to handle or to eat. These animals usually have bright colours warning others not to touch them.

Cryptic

Hiding by using the colours of the surroundings is called cryptic camouflage. Cryptic comes from a Greek word meaning 'hidden'. Other animals look like dangerous animals, but are just copying their colours to try to frighten enemies away.

The hunters use camouflage to get as near to their prey as possible before striking. Some hunters look like harmless fishes until the prey approaches.

There is also the camouflage due to an animal being able to change its colours, like a chameleon, except that many fishes can do this far better than any chameleon.

Stripes, bands and spots are also camouflage. They break up the outline of the body so the fish blends with the background.

No camouflage is completely successful. As a rule it is no longer of use the moment the animal moves. Even so, it is very important to animals. Apart from anything else, it helps them to hide while they are resting or sleeping.

Natural Selection

Animals get these colours and colour patterns by what is called natural selection. In any brood of animal babies the colours and the patterns differ slightly from one to the other. One baby will, when it grows up, look more like its habitat, that is the place where it lives, than another. It will, as a result, stand a better chance of not being killed. In other words, Nature selects those with the more suitable colours or colour patterns, to live, grow up and have their own babies.

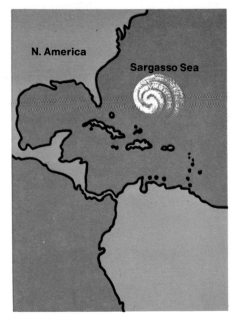

N. America

Sargasso Sea

The Sargasso Sea is in the Atlantic, off the coast of America (see left). It was given its name because of the masses of floating seaweed found there. People used to say that ships could not plough through this seaweed because there was so much of it. This is not true, but there is a great deal of seaweed there. It is of a special kind. It has tiny bladders that help it to float. The weed is carried by the Gulf Stream, a current, into the North Atlantic. The Gulf Stream currents go round and round at the Sargasso Sea. They form what is called a vortex. This piles the weed at the centre.

Scientists have always been interested in the Sargasso Sea, but they still do not have all the answers. It has, however, been there a very long time. Some animals have been able to adapt themselves to this special life. A fish called the Sargassum fish (see below) looks very like the Sargassum weed in colour and shape. It is very difficult to see among the weed. The Sargassum fish lays eggs among the weed which are about the same size and colour as the bladders on the weed.

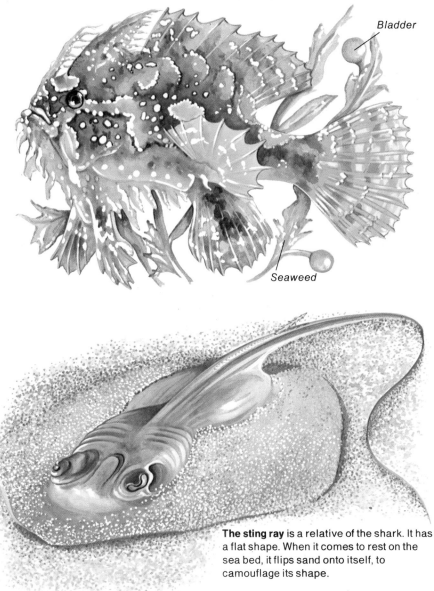

Bladder

Seaweed

The sting ray is a relative of the shark. It has a flat shape. When it comes to rest on the sea bed, it flips sand onto itself, to camouflage its shape.

Inside a Fish

A fish is completely adapted to life underwater. It has just the simple organs and muscles which it needs.

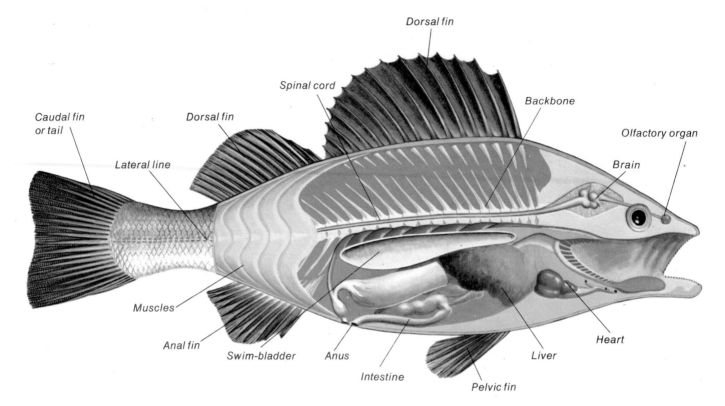

Dorsal fin

Spinal cord

Backbone

Olfactory organ

Brain

Caudal fin or tail

Dorsal fin

Lateral line

Muscles

Anal fin

Swim-bladder

Anus

Intestine

Pelvic fin

Liver

Heart

Swim Bladder

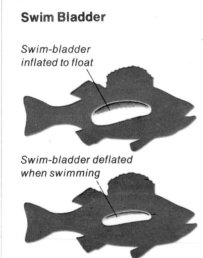

Swim-bladder inflated to float

Swim-bladder deflated when swimming

The swim-bladder is a float which, when blown up, or inflated, stops a fish from sinking when it is not swimming. It acts rather like a life-jacket in giving floating-power, or buoyancy. Not all fishes have a swim-bladder. Deep sea fishes, and large, fast-swimming fishes, like the tuna, have an oily flesh that keeps them afloat. Sharks have an oily liver. Fishes that live on the sea bed, like plaice, do not need a float.

A fish has a backbone made up of separate pieces of bone, called vertebrae. The largest nerve of its body, called the spinal cord, runs through the backbone. The spinal cord gets bigger at the front of the fish, and forms the brain. Nerves run out from the brain to the eyes, nostrils, and other sense organs. Other nerves go to the face. Pairs of nerves lead off all along the spinal cord to other parts of the body. Nerves carry messages to and from the brain. Underneath the backbone are all the other organs of the body—the stomach, intestine, heart and blood vessels. The long, silvery bag in the middle of the organs is the swim-bladder.

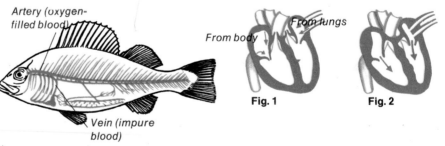

Artery (oxygen-filled blood)

Vein (impure blood)

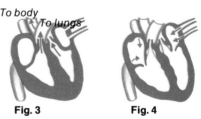

From lungs

From body

Fig. 1

Fig. 2

To body

To lungs

Fig. 3

Fig. 4

The heart of a fish is just a simple pump. It pushes the blood round and round the body, and over the gills. There, the blood takes in oxygen from the water the fish breathes in. In man, the heart is more complicated. Impure blood from the body comes to the heart in veins (Fig. 1). At the same time, pure blood comes from the lungs, where it has collected oxygen. Both types of blood are pumped separately through the heart (Fig. 2). The impure blood goes to the lungs to collect oxygen, and the pure blood goes to the body (Fig. 3). The impure blood that was pumped to the lungs comes back as pure blood, and the pure blood comes back impure from the body (Fig. 4). Then the process begins again (Fig. 1).

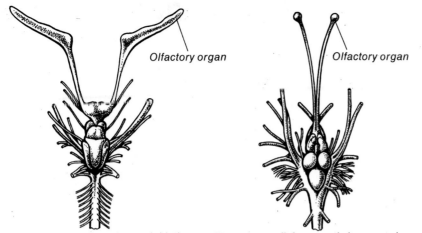

Sharks and rays, with a skeleton of gristle, or cartilage, have poor eyesight. They depend very much on their sense of smell. Experts know this because they have studied their brain. The parts which deal with the sense of smell—the olfactory organs—are very large.

Bony, or true fishes mostly have good eyesight. The part of the brain dealing with sight is larger than in the brain of a shark. Also, the olfactory organs are small. This means the bony fishes cannot smell as well as sharks, but they can see better.

Taste and Sight

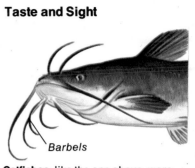

Barbels

Catfishes, like the one above, were given their name because of the whiskers on their snout. These whiskers are special organs of taste. The sense of taste is usually in the tongue, in groups of tiny cells called taste-buds. Some fishes have taste buds all over their body. Catfishes have them especially on their 'whiskers'.

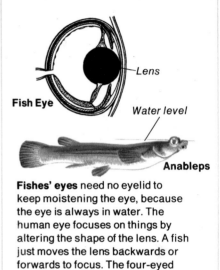

Fish Eye — Lens — Water level — **Anableps**

Fishes' eyes need no eyelid to keep moistening the eye, because the eye is always in water. The human eye focuses on things by altering the shape of the lens. A fish just moves the lens backwards or forwards to focus. The four-eyed fish, Anableps, swims with one-half of each eye above the water, so it can see in air and water.

Fishes have a sort of sixth sense. It is called the lateral line. Lateral means on the side, and the lateral line can be clearly seen on the side of many fishes as a line of scales running from just behind the gills to the base of the tail fin. This lateral line can detect movement in the water around the fish. A fish can tell if another animal is swimming towards it.

A tube runs along the lateral line. In the middle of each scale is a tiny opening. Inside the tube are many very small sense organs. They pick up vibrations in the surrounding water.

The Body of a Fish

Inside, a fish has in general the same organs as any other backboned animal. There are a few differences. Fishes have gills instead of lungs, and fins instead of legs. These fins are specially adapted to balance the fish as it swims along. The long, cylindrical shape allows the fish to move easily through the water. The heart is just a simple pump to keep the blood flowing. In fast-swimming fishes, most of the body is made up of muscle. The internal organs take up a very small space.

Cold Blood

Fishes are cold-blooded. This means that they do not have a steady body temperature, like warm-blooded creatures. The temperature of a fish changes with the temperature of the water. If that temperature changes suddenly, the fish could die.

However, water is a poor conductor of heat, so the temperature of water changes very slowly. A cold-blooded fish is safe.

Movement and Energy

When a land animal runs, or a bird flies, a lot of energy is used up. The blood must be pumped faster to make this good. A fish slips easily through water. Its shape is right for easy movement. Not much energy is needed. The skin is also covered with a layer of slime, called mucus, which comes from skin glands. This lubricates the skin, making it slippery so that the fish can slide through the water without effort.

Salt

The body of a freshwater fish has more salt in it than the surrounding water. This draws water in through its skin. So the fish does not need to drink. A saltwater fish has less salt than its surroundings. All the time water is being drawn out of its body into the surrounding salt water. So it has to drink large quantities.

The Food Chain

There is a food chain, or web, underwater. Each link depends on the next for survival.

Chlorophyll

Energy comes from the sun. Plants contain a green substance, called chlorophyll (klo-ro-fil). With chlorophyll they make sugars and starch to produce energy, with the help of the sun's rays.

Some animals feed only on plants. They are called plant-eaters, or herbivores. Other animals eat the herbivores. They are called flesh-eaters, or carnivores. There are other plants and animals that eat dead plants and animals, or the waste from animals. They are called scavengers.

Sea Plants

In the sea there is a vast amount of plant life. There are the seaweeds. Some are tiny, others are 100 feet (30 metres) long. Seaweeds, however, only live round the coasts, except in the Sargasso Sea. 99 per cent of plant life in the sea is made up of tiny microscopic floating

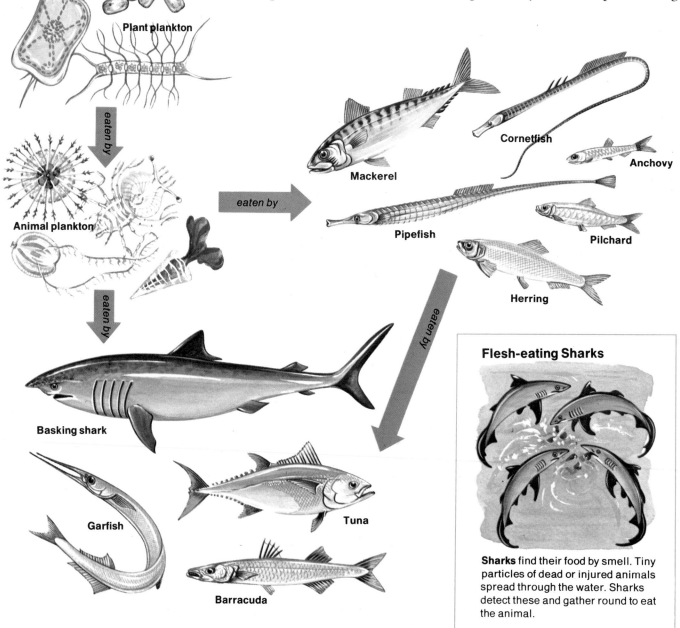

Surface of sea

Plant plankton

eaten by

Animal plankton

eaten by

eaten by

Mackerel

Cornetfish

Anchovy

Pipefish

Pilchard

Herring

eaten by

Basking shark

Garfish

Tuna

Barracuda

Flesh-eating Sharks

Sharks find their food by smell. Tiny particles of dead or injured animals spread through the water. Sharks detect these and gather round to eat the animal.

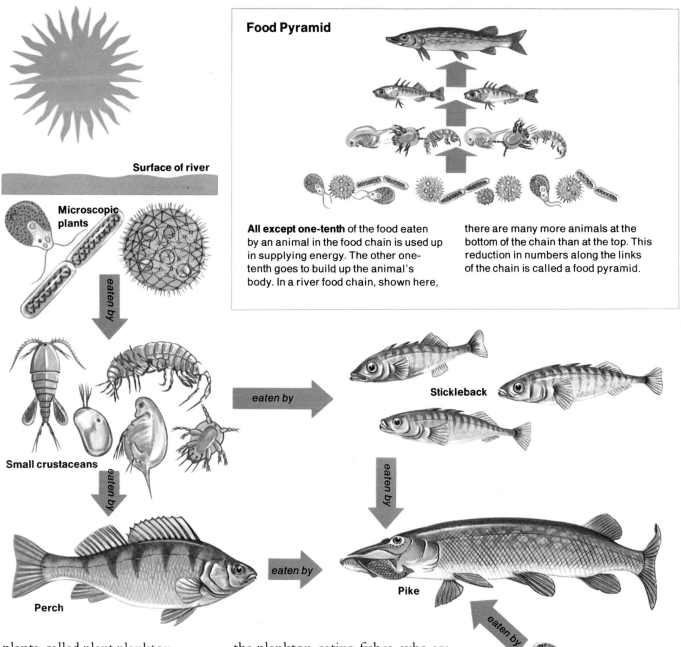

Food Pyramid

Surface of river

Microscopic plants

eaten by

Small crustaceans

eaten by

Perch

eaten by

Stickleback

eaten by

Pike

eaten by

All except one-tenth of the food eaten by an animal in the food chain is used up in supplying energy. The other one-tenth goes to build up the animal's body. In a river food chain, shown here, there are many more animals at the bottom of the chain than at the top. This reduction in numbers along the links of the chain is called a food pyramid.

plants, called plant plankton.

Animals
There are also many tiny animals. Some can just be seen with the naked eye. These feed on the plants, and the larger animals also eat the smaller ones. They are all called the animal plankton. Fishes like the herring, mackerel and pilchard feed on animal plankton. These in turn are eaten by larger fishes like the tuna, and also by dolphins and porpoises.

Food Chain
This is known as a food chain. The plant plankton is eaten by the animal plankton, which is eaten by the plankton-eating fishes, who are eaten by fish–eating fishes.

Sharks
The plant and animal plankton is eaten not only by the small fishes, but also by two of the largest. These are the basking shark, which is 40 feet (12 metres) long, and the whale shark, up to 55 feet (17 metres) long. These two huge sharks just open their enormous mouths, gulp in water and strain the plankton through their gill-rakers.

River Life
The food chain of a river (above) works in the same way as for the sea, but there are more large plants.

Frog

The pike is at the top of the food pyramid in a stream. It will eat not only fishes, but also anything else it can catch—frogs, for example. A pike will also eat a water bird, or even an otter.

Courting and Nesting

Most fishes do not really woo a mate. Some, however, have special courtship dances, and even build nests.

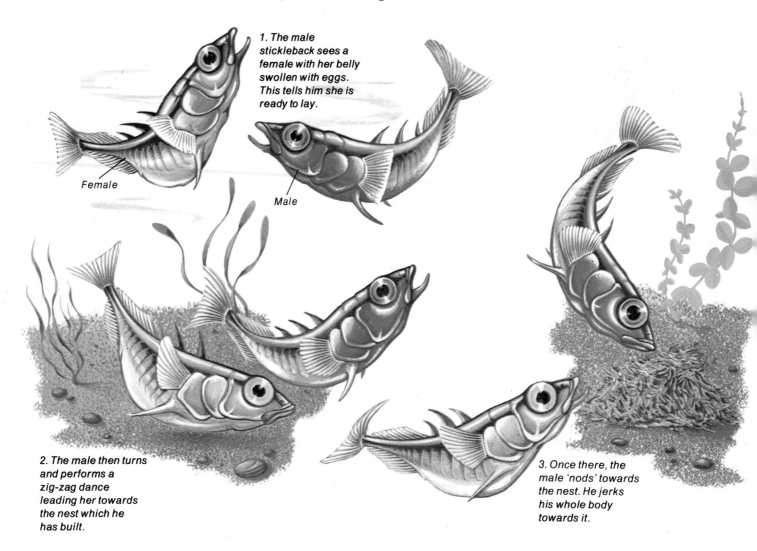

1. The male stickleback sees a female with her belly swollen with eggs. This tells him she is ready to lay.

Female

Male

2. The male then turns and performs a zig-zag dance leading her towards the nest which he has built.

3. Once there, the male 'nods' towards the nest. He jerks his whole body towards it.

Mating

The mating season is not the same for all animals. Mating always takes place, however, in time for the babies to be born when food is most plentiful. Usually, the length of day and temperature of water tell fishes when the breeding season has arrived. Eggs are laid by the female. They are fertilized by sperms from the male. In some animals, this happens inside the female. Fishes, however, usually just shed their eggs and sperms into the water when they mate.

Courtship

Some fishes make nests. These fishes usually have an elaborate courtship. The males put on brighter colours. The throat and breast of the male stickleback turn red. He is then called a red throat.

Fishes can feel even very small vibrations in water. Male fishes that are rivals for territory beat their tails at each other. This must send strong vibrations through the water. Sometimes tail-beating is used to court the female.

Some courting fishes swim round each other in an excited way that is quite different from their usual calm way of swimming. They almost perform a dance, with the male raising all his fins.

Mating for Life?

It is not known whether any fishes pair for life, but it may be true that some do. The most that is known is that once a pair has mated, the two are likely to come together again.

Nests

Not many fishes make actual nests. The stickleback does. It uses pieces of weed. But often a nest is just a shallow pit in the sandy bed of a lake or stream. The fish uses its mouth as a scoop to carry the sand away. Freshwater fishes that lay their eggs direct onto a stone will spend a lot of time cleaning the surface, using their mouths.

Tail-beating and Nest-building

Velvet cichlids use tail-beating in courtship. They drive small currents of water at each other by moving their tails.

The tilapia fish digs a pit for its eggs by scooping out sand with its mouth on the bed of a lake.

Lampreys use their sucker mouths to make a wall of stones. This stops the eggs being swept downstream by the current.

4. The female enters the nest. The male nudges her flank, or side, with his snout to make her lay.

5. When she has laid her eggs the male drives her out through the other side of the nest.

6. He then goes into the nest and sheds his milt over the eggs. Milt is the sperm from the male which fertilizes the eggs so that they will grow into fishes.

7. The male now stays near the nest to tend the eggs. With his fins he fans fresh water into the nest. Soon the eggs will hatch and his job will be finished.

27

How are Fishes Born?

All fishes lay eggs of one kind or another. The eggs are protected in many different ways.

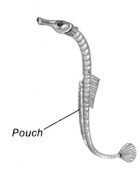

Pouch

The male and female pipefish come together to mate.

The female lays her eggs in a pouch on the male's belly.

The eggs stay in the male's pouch until they hatch.

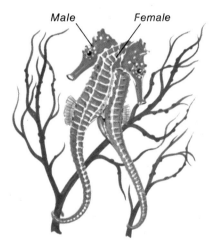

Male   Female

Pouch

Seahorses are very like pipefishes in their behaviour. The female lays her eggs in the male's pouch.

The female leaves the male to bear the baby seahorses.

These baby seahorses are about a day old. They are able to look after themselves.

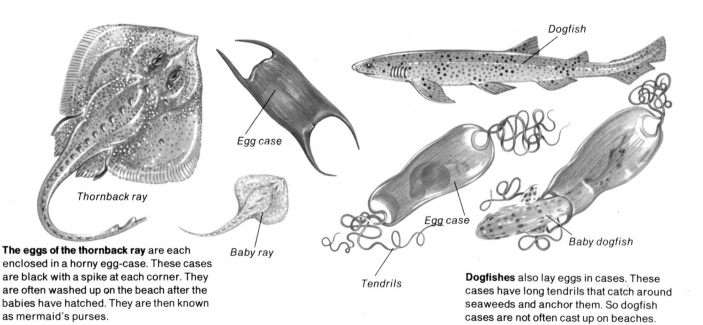

Thornback ray

Egg case

Baby ray

Tendrils

Dogfish

Egg case

Baby dogfish

The eggs of the thornback ray are each enclosed in a horny egg-case. These cases are black with a spike at each corner. They are often washed up on the beach after the babies have hatched. They are then known as mermaid's purses.

Dogfishes also lay eggs in cases. These cases have long tendrils that catch around seaweeds and anchor them. So dogfish cases are not often cast up on beaches.

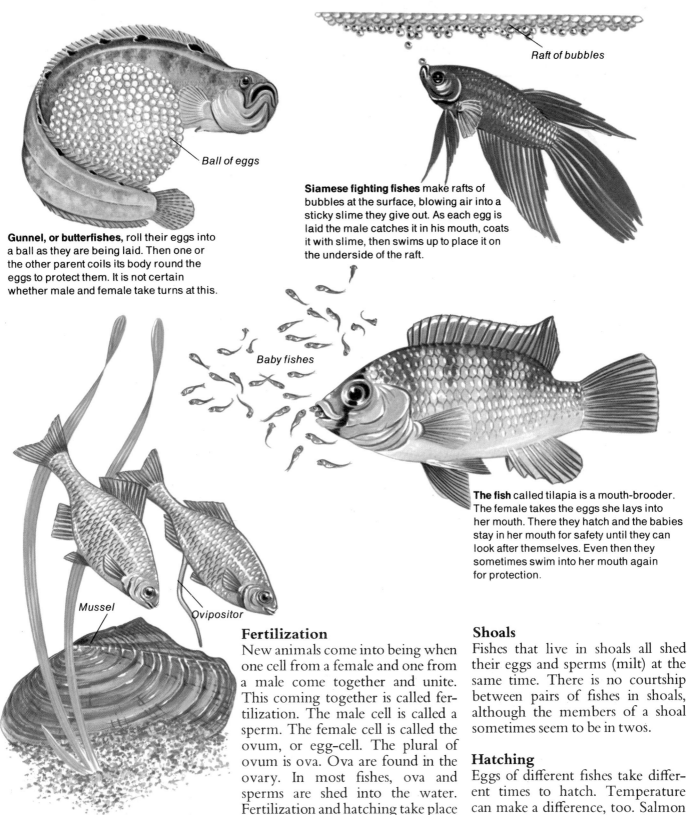

Gunnel, or butterfishes, roll their eggs into a ball as they are being laid. Then one or the other parent coils its body round the eggs to protect them. It is not certain whether male and female take turns at this.

Ball of eggs

Raft of bubbles

Siamese fighting fishes make rafts of bubbles at the surface, blowing air into a sticky slime they give out. As each egg is laid the male catches it in his mouth, coats it with slime, then swims up to place it on the underside of the raft.

Baby fishes

Mussel

Ovipositor

The fish called tilapia is a mouth-brooder. The female takes the eggs she lays into her mouth. There they hatch and the babies stay in her mouth for safety until they can look after themselves. Even then they sometimes swim into her mouth again for protection.

In the breeding season the female bitterling grows a long ovipositor, or egg-laying tube. She lays her eggs in a freshwater mussel. As she does this the male sheds his milt on them. The eggs are safe inside the mussel. At the same time the mussel ejects its larvae which cling to the bitterling's skin and are carried about by her.

Fertilization

New animals come into being when one cell from a female and one from a male come together and unite. This coming together is called fertilization. The male cell is called a sperm. The female cell is called the ovum, or egg-cell. The plural of ovum is ova. Ova are found in the ovary. In most fishes, ova and sperms are shed into the water. Fertilization and hatching take place in the water. In a small number of fishes, the male places his sperms inside the female's body, and the fertilized eggs hatch there. The babies are born alive. This is an actual mating, sometimes called coupling, or copulation.

Shoals

Fishes that live in shoals all shed their eggs and sperms (milt) at the same time. There is no courtship between pairs of fishes in shoals, although the members of a shoal sometimes seem to be in twos.

Hatching

Eggs of different fishes take different times to hatch. Temperature can make a difference, too. Salmon eggs hatch in 90 days at 8°C and 114 days at 3°C. Eggs of some small tropical fishes hatch in one to two days. Trout eggs take as much as five months. As a rule, the larger the fish, the longer the time needed for the eggs to hatch.

Growing Up

Fishes, like other animals, have to grow up. Sometimes the young of a fish look quite different from the adult.

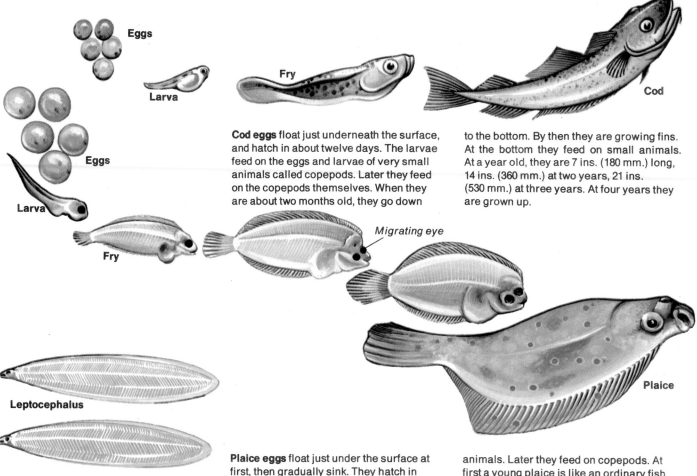

Cod eggs float just underneath the surface, and hatch in about twelve days. The larvae feed on the eggs and larvae of very small animals called copepods. Later they feed on the copepods themselves. When they are about two months old, they go down to the bottom. By then they are growing fins. At the bottom they feed on small animals. At a year old, they are 7 ins. (180 mm.) long, 14 ins. (360 mm.) at two years, 21 ins. (530 mm.) at three years. At four years they are grown up.

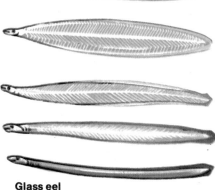

Plaice eggs float just under the surface at first, then gradually sink. They hatch in three weeks, and the larvae are $\frac{1}{4}$ in. (6.5 mm.) long. At first they eat nothing, then they start to eat diatoms (microscopic plants) and very tiny larvae of small animals. Later they feed on copepods. At first a young plaice is like an ordinary fish, but when it is 40 days old and $\frac{1}{2}$ in. (13 mm.) long it begins to turn onto its left side. At the same time the left eye migrates through the skull and comes to lie near the right eye.

Eel larvae are so unlike their parents that for a long time they were thought to belong to a different species. They were given the name leptocephalus (plural: leptocephali), meaning very small head. The body is three ins. (75 mm.) long, flat and leaf-shaped. They migrate from the mid-Atlantic to the coasts of America and Europe. During this time the body becomes rounder and thinner. When they reach the coast, they change into young eels, or elvers. Another name for an elver is glass eel, because the eel is almost as transparent as the water it swims in.

How Long is a Lifetime?

There are fishes called annual fishes that live in South America and Africa. They hatch, grow up, lay their eggs and die in under a year. Most fishes live much longer. There is a story of a pike that lived for 267 years, but there is no proof of this. Probably the pike did not live more than 60 or 70 years. There are stories of carp living to 150 years, but 50 years is probably the most they reach. Most fishes live much shorter lives, but it is difficult to say exactly how long their lives are.

Life and Death

Many fishes die young. A herring will lay up to 50,000 eggs, a plaice up to 500,000 and a cod up to 7 million. The record is held by a large ling that laid over 28 million eggs. Not all these eggs hatch. Many animals feed on fish eggs and larvae and fry, and there are many others that feed on young fishes. On average, only one out of these large totals of eggs will survive long enough to breed. If this were not so, there would soon be no room for all the fishes.

Freshwater Fishes

Freshwater fishes lay only hundreds or scores of eggs. Many fishes bear live young. They have a better chance of survival because as eggs they are protected inside the mother's body.

Scales and Spines

Scales are a protection for the fish's skin. Some fishes even have spines and armour to protect them.

Shark

The skin of a shark is like sandpaper. Instead of flat scales it is covered with little teeth, called denticles. They are scales of a type known as placoid.

Scales

There are a few fishes that have no scales. They have a tough, leathery skin instead, like the catfishes and the conger eels. Most fishes have delicate skin which would quickly be damaged without the protective scales. There are many shapes and sizes of scales. The tarpon, a large marine fish 6½ feet (2 metres) or more long, has scales two inches (50 mm.) across. The mahseer, a game fish living in the rivers of India has scales as large as a man's palm. The common eel has scales so small they can only be seen under a microscope.

Some scales are set firmly in the skin, as in the plaice. In other fishes, the scales are in such shallow pockets that they are easily rubbed off when handled. This sort of scale is called a deciduous scale, from the Latin word meaning 'to fall'. The sardine, pilchard, herring and sprat have these deciduous scales.

Bichir

A few fishes, like the bichir of Africa, have ganoid scales. These fit together just like a mosaic. Many extinct fishes had scales of this kind, and the bichir is a sort of living fossil.

Sawfish

Puffer fish

Trunkfish

Perch

A perch has scales with little teeth on the end, like a comb. They are called ctenoid (tee-noid) scales.

Scales are a protective covering for a fish. Sometimes they are a kind of armour. The trunkfish has scales that fit neatly together to form a bony box. It can only move its tail and fins for swimming. The porcupine fish or puffer fish is covered with spines. It can blow itself up with air. The scales then stand up. The sawfish has a long, flat snout, with a row of 'teeth' that are really scales along each side.

Carp

Bony fishes usually have scales that overlap, like tiles on a roof. They are called cycloid scales.

Scales

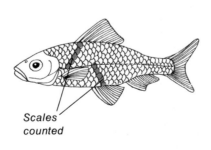

Scales counted

Some species of fishes are so alike it is difficult to tell them apart. The scientist must then count the scales. He counts the rows downwards and forwards from the dorsal fin to the lateral line, and from the lateral line to the pelvic fin.

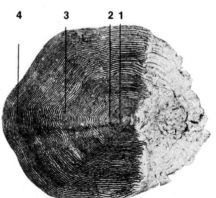

4   3   2 1

Scientists can identify fishes by looking at their scales. Sometimes, they can also tell the age of a fish. Some scales (see above) have annual rings, like the trunk of a tree. A count of these rings gives the fish's age.

Journey of a Lifetime

Some fishes make long migrations. Eels live in freshwater, but go to the sea to spawn. Salmon do just the opposite.

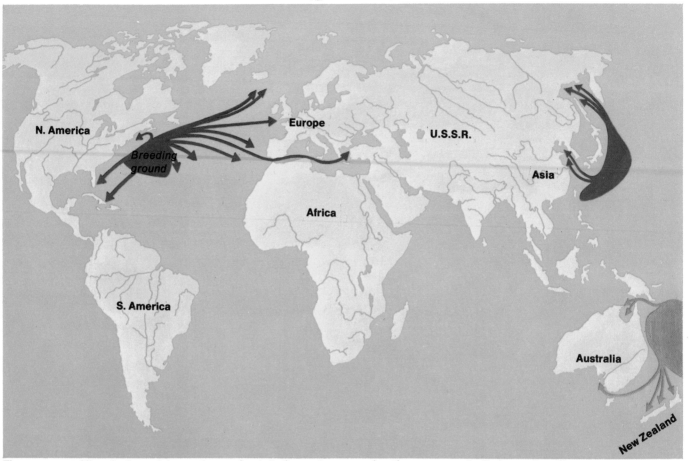

The common eel lives in rivers, lakes and ponds, even in coastal waters of the sea. For years it feeds and grows. It may be more than five ft. (1.5 m.) long. The males do not live as far inland as the females. The males migrate to the sea to spawn when they are eight to ten years old. The females do the same, but at ten to 18 years of age. This migration takes place each autumn. The eels swim across the Atlantic to a place south of the Sargasso Sea. There they spawn and die. The eggs float at about 1,300 ft. (400 m.) below the surface. Eels in eastern Asia, Australia and New Zealand make similar migrations.

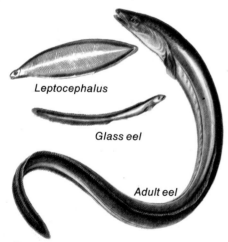

Leptocephalus

Glass eel

Adult eel

The young or larvae from eels' eggs are called leptocephali. They return to the waters their parents came from. They gradually change into elvers, or glass eels. These go up the rivers, often moving overland to lakes, to feed.

The Life of an Eel

Eels spend most of their lives in rivers and lakes, then go down to the sea to spawn.

There are three stages to their development. The larvae, or baby eels, are thin and flat, and are called leptocphali (lep-to-kef-ali). For a long time, people did not know that leptocephali were baby eels, because they look so different from adult eels.

The leptocephali gradually make their way across the sea towards the rivers. They change into elvers, or young eels. They are often called glass eels. The eels grow to be adult, and spend most of their adult life in the rivers. Then they change into silver eels, and make for the sea, to spawn just like their parents did. This journey is called a breeding migration.

The Last Journey

Their eyes grow very big, like those of some deep sea fishes, as they go back to the sea. This migration happens every autumn. The eels swim from Europe and America to the deep seas in mid-Atlantic. There they lay their eggs, fertilize them, and then die.

Eels are caught for market in traps, eel-pots, or by line. The young elvers also used to be caught when ascending rivers in spring. Their migrations, in vast numbers, were called eel fares.

The Life History of the Salmon

Eggs are laid on gravel beds of small streams

Eggs hatch into alevins. → Yolk

Salmon fry, or fingerlings, 4–6 weeks old

Parr marks

Parr are 4–8 ins. (100–200 mm.) long and head for the sea.

Feeding ground

The Atlantic salmon is found in the rivers flowing into the North Atlantic, but it spends most of its life in the sea. Its feeding grounds are to the south of Greenland. When fully grown and ready to spawn, the salmon makes its way back to the same river in which it was hatched.

A male salmon returns upstream to spawn

Hooked lower jaw

To the sea →

Smolts may be 3–7 years old before they reach the sea

On their way back upstream, to spawn, salmon leap high out of the water to pass weirs and waterfalls. Sometimes, concrete steps, called ladders, are built for them so they can bypass obstacles like hydro-electric stations and dams.

Story of the Salmon

Salmon breed in rivers, but live in the sea. The baby salmon, called alevins, hatch and feed on what is left of the egg-yolk. After a month or so, they begin to eat insect larvae. They are now called fry, or finger-lings. They start making their way downstream to the sea.

After about two years, they are four to eight inches (100–200 mm.) long, with crossmarks, called parr marks, on their bodies. Two years later they lose the parr marks, and become shining silver smolts. They may be three to seven years old before they reach the sea. There they feed for three or four years.

Then they start their long journey back to spawn in the stream in which they were hatched. They find their way by the sun and stars. Once at the coast, they pick up the taste of the water from their birthplace, and follow it upstream.

Change

Their colour changes to reddish-brown, with red and black spots. The lower jaw of the male turns up in a hook at the tip.

The salmon do not eat on this journey. After they have spawned, they go back down river. Many die on the way. A few reach the sea, thin and weak. There they soon fatten up, and may later return upstream to spawn again.

33

Fishes of the Deeps

Some fishes live down in the cold and darkness of the ocean deeps. Many of them are very strange.

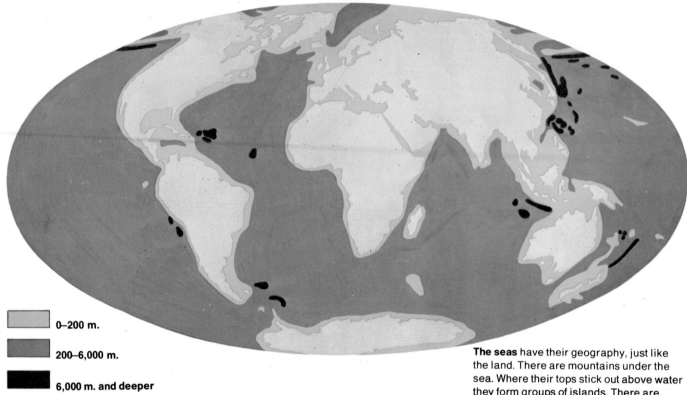

0–200 m.

200–6,000 m.

6,000 m. and deeper

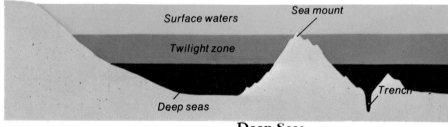

Surface waters

Sea mount

Twilight zone

Deep seas

Trench

The seas have their geography, just like the land. There are mountains under the sea. Where their tops stick out above water they form groups of islands. There are mountain ranges under the sea, and deep trenches. The deepest trench is the Mariana Trench in the Pacific. It is 35,640 ft. (10,863 m.) deep. This is higher than Mount Everest. In the oceans there are surface waters (the first 300 ft. or 100 m.), and bottom waters with mid-waters in between. There is a twilight zone from 1,600 ft.-3,000 ft. (500 m.-1,000 m.). Below that is eternal darkness.

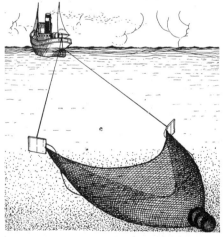

This is the sort of net to haul up specimens of fishes from mid-waters. One of the problems of finding specimens is to know exactly what depth they live at. They may have got into the net as it was hauled up. This kind of net is called a trawl.

Deep Seas

The water is cold in the deeps and the animals are more spaced out than in the warmer waters above. There is a shortage of food in the deeps. Some fishes feed on the bodies of small animals that have died in the surface waters and drifted down. Many deep-sea fishes feed on other fishes that have eaten these dead animals. There is also a third kind, like the lantern fishes, that come up into the surface layers at night to feed.

Light Organs

Many deep-sea fishes have lights on their bodies which shine in the darkness. They attract other animals, which are then snapped up.

The lights also help the fishes to recognise others of their own kind, especially for mating. Usually, fishes with lights have large eyes. They need these to recognise each other in the dark. But some have small eyes or even no eyes at all. They have special senses for feeling their way around.

Pressure

The weight of all the water above causes great pressure in the deeps. This is too great for man to stand, but it is no problem for the fishes. They are adapted to high pressures. They do not live long when brought up from the deeps. This means it is very difficult to study them.

Hatchet fishes are usually less than six ins. (150 mm.) long. They have large eyes compared with the size of their body. They live at between 300 ft. and 1,600 ft. (100 m.-500 m.) depth.

Ipnops lives at a depth of 13,000 ft. (4,000 m.). It has no eyes, probably because it lives in the darkest depths, where there is no light. Little is known about its way of life.

Opisthoproctus is a deep-sea fish from the mid-waters, about 2½ ins. (60 mm.) long. It has tubular eyes which give it good distant and nearby vision.

Anglerfishes have a long spine with a light at the end to lure prey into the mouth. Some male deep-sea anglerfishes are very much smaller than the female. They fasten onto the female, and stay there for the rest of their lives.

Gulper eels live at depths of 1,600 ft. to 6,500 ft. (500 m. to 2,000 m.) or more. They can measure six ft. or more (about 2 m.) long. They have enormous jaws for swallowing fishes larger than themselves. Food is hard to come by in the depths, and a meal has to last a long time.

Vinciguerria lives at depths of 300 ft. to 1,600 ft. (100 m. to 500 m.). It has rows of light organs along its sides, like the portholes of a ship. It probably uses these lights to look for food.

Light is made by changing one sort of energy into another. The light a bulb gives off is a warm light. The light is only 14% of the energy produced. The other 86% is given off as heat. The lights of the deep-sea fishes are cold, so no energy is lost.

Lantern fishes are so-called because they have lots of lights. They come up to the surface at night to feed on prawns and small fishes. They return to their home, about 1,600 ft. (500 m.) down, at dawn.

Tropical Fishes

Many beautiful and brightly-coloured fishes flourish in the warm waters of the Tropics.

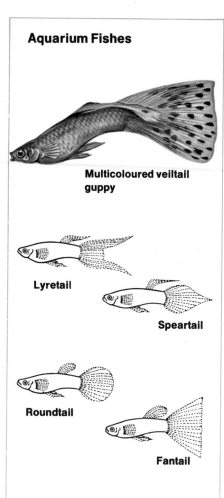

Aquarium Fishes

Multicoloured veiltail guppy

Lyretail

Speartail

Roundtail

Fantail

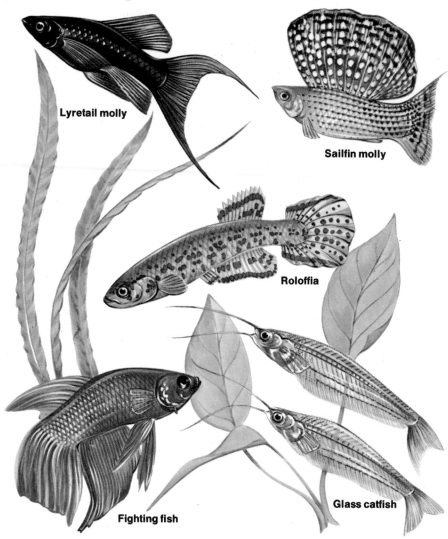

Lyretail molly

Sailfin molly

Roloffia

Glass catfish

Fighting fish

Tropical fishes are often kept in an aquarium. An aquarium is a water-tight glass box, like a miniature lake. The guppy, above, is one of the favourite aquarium fishes. It has been specially bred for a long time to produce many different varieties.

An aquarium for tropical fishes must be lit with a special electric light by day, and it must always be heated. Usually, an electric heater is immersed in the water. This is controlled by a thermostat. The thermostat keeps the temperature of the water steady at around 21°C.

Many of the smaller tropical fishes, especially those living in streams and lakes, are beautifully coloured. Some of the great favourites are far more beautiful than the fishes from which they have been bred. The wild fighting fish is a greyish green, quite unlike the magnificent purple or red aquarium fighting fish.

Sunshine

In the Tropics, there is more sunshine and the days are warmer than in temperate regions. The flowers are larger and more brightly coloured. The fishes and other animals of the rivers and seas are also brighter. It is hard to say why, except that colour seems to have something to do with the amount of sunshine. Not all tropical fishes are brightly coloured, but many are.

Camouflage

Surprisingly, these bright colours are usually camouflage. There are good examples of this on the coral reefs. These have sometimes been called Gardens of the Sea. The coral animals themselves are brilliant reds, purples, greens and yellows. If the fishes living round the reefs had dull colours, they could quickly be seen. The bright colours, or patches of bright colour on their bodies, match the colours of the corals.

This is not always so. Some coral reefs are drab, yet the fishes living around them are brightly coloured. They do not need camouflage. They rely on speed for protection. When danger appears, they dart swiftly into the crevices and crannies in the coral. As a rule, in tropical fishes and others as well, the colours fade at night after the sun has gone down.

The fishes above are freshwater tropicals. Those on page 37 are marine.

Jigsaw triggerfish

Moorish idol

Koran angelfish
(young)

Royal gramma

Picasso fish

Black clownfish

Emperor angelfish

French angelfish

Banded pipefish

Common clownfish

Sea anemone

Queen triggerfish

Poison and Electricity

Some fishes protect themselves from their enemies, and perhaps catch their prey, by using poison or electricity.

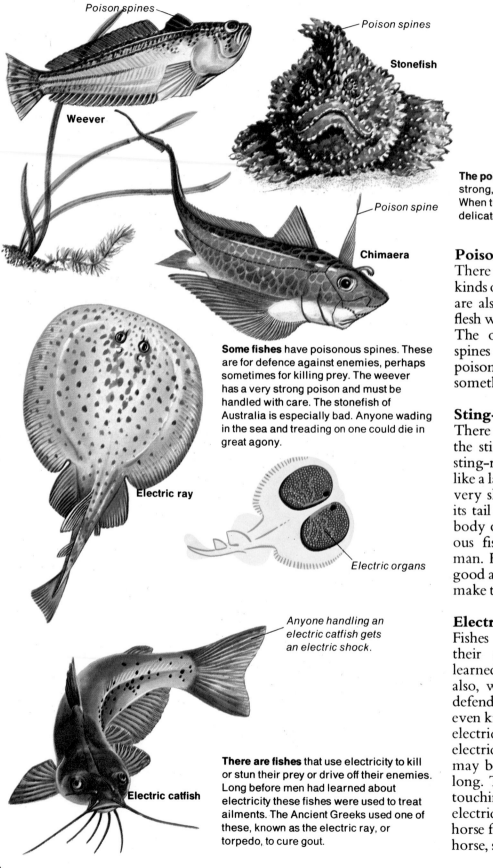

Poison spines

Weever

Poison spines

Stonefish

Poison spine

Chimaera

Poison sac

Spine

The poison spine is a fin-ray, specially strong, with a poison gland. It is grooved. When the spine is touched this breaks the delicate skin covering it.

Some fishes have poisonous spines. These are for defence against enemies, perhaps sometimes for killing prey. The weever has a very strong poison and must be handled with care. The stonefish of Australia is especially bad. Anyone wading in the sea and treading on one could die in great agony.

Electric ray

Electric organs

Anyone handling an electric catfish gets an electric shock.

Electric catfish

There are fishes that use electricity to kill or stun their prey or drive off their enemies. Long before men had learned about electricity these fishes were used to treat ailments. The Ancient Greeks used one of these, known as the electric ray, or torpedo, to cure gout.

Poison
There are at least 50 different kinds of fishes that use poison. There are also fishes that have poisonous flesh which can kill anyone eating it. The other poisonous fishes have spines with poison glands. The poison, as a rule, does not work until something touches one of the spines.

Sting-ray
There are, however, a few, such as the sting-ray, that strike out. The sting-ray has a dagger-like spine, like a large tooth, near the base of its very slender tail. It can whip with its tail and drive the spine into the body of an attacker. Some poisonous fishes are very dangerous to man. For most of them there is no good antidote, that is, a medicine to make the poison harmless.

Electric Shockers
Fishes were using poison against their enemies long before man learned to do so. Some of them, also, were using electric shocks to defend themselves long before men even knew there was such a thing as electricity. The most famous is the electric eel of South America. This may be nine feet (2.7 m.) or more long. Touching one of these is like touching a bare light switch. An electric eel touching the legs of a horse fording a river will throw the horse, stunned by the shock.

Flying and Talking

Flying fishes can leap out of the water and glide for long distances. Some fishes can communicate with each other.

The manta ray measures up to 20 ft. (6 m.) across, and lives in tropical seas. Sometimes it leaps high out of the water. It looks like a huge bat.

A flying fish swims quickly up to the surface. As its body leaves the water, its tail goes from side to side to keep it moving until it has spread its fins to catch the air. Once airborne it glides (see below). The air currents may lift the fish as much as 20 ft. (6 m.). Flying fishes sometimes land on the decks of ships. The flying fish can glide up to a quarter of a mile (400 m.), and reach speeds of 40 m.p.h. (64 k.p.h.).

Flying

There are plenty of fishes that will jump out of the water as easily as a man can jump into it. Some, like the garfishes, seem to do so for fun. A garfish has been seen to jump over a floating log, and do a somersault as it did so. The garfish is closely related to the flying fishes. If it had larger fins it would be able to glide, once it was clear of the water, just as flying fishes do. Flying fishes do not truly fly. They glide. To do this they leap from the water, and waggle the tail along in the water. This is called taxi-ing. Then, when the spread fins have got enough lift, the fishes become airborne.

Talking

When a person talks he is passing his ideas to another person. This is called communicating his thoughts. No fish can talk. Many use communication and a large number of them use sounds for this. They may make sounds by grinding their teeth together, not the teeth in their jaws but the special throat teeth many fishes have. Others rub their gill covers or rub the spines in their fins together, or they may rub some of the small bones in their heads together. Many fishes have a swim-bladder containing a gas. This gives them buoyancy. Some fishes use muscles to pluck the taut surface of the swim-bladder to drum.

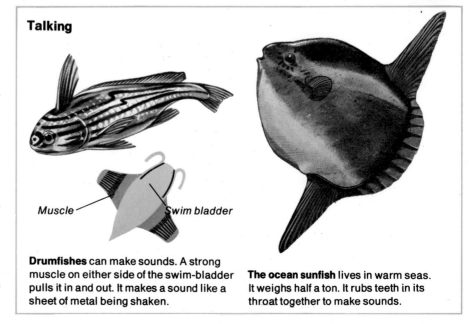

Talking

Muscle — *Swim bladder*

Drumfishes can make sounds. A strong muscle on either side of the swim-bladder pulls it in and out. It makes a sound like a sheet of metal being shaken.

The ocean sunfish lives in warm seas. It weighs half a ton. It rubs teeth in its throat together to make sounds.

Friends and Enemies

Sometimes, two different fishes will live together in a partnership, which benefits one or both. Other fishes do not have this arrangement.

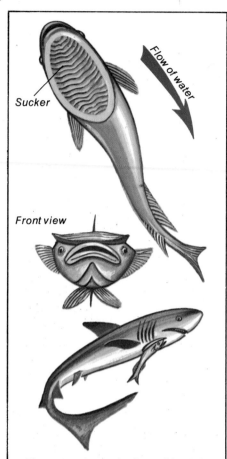

The remora uses sharks or ships to ride about the ocean. Its other name is shark-sucker. What should have been its dorsal fin has been changed into a large oval sucker, covering the top of the head. The remora can only be moved once it has stuck onto something by moving it forwards. So no matter how fast the shark swims, the remora cannot be washed off.

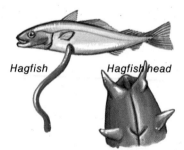

The hagfish is a jawless fish. It fastens itself to the body of another fish by boring into its side with its rasp-like tongue. It eats away the flesh. In the end, only skin and bones are left. The hagfish is therefore a parasite, but it only lives off dying fishes.

The small, striped fish in this picture is called a barber fish, or a cleaner fish. It works over the body of other, larger fishes, cleaning them up by removing small skin parasites and pieces of dead skin. Barbers eat what they clean off. They have special places where they station themselves. Fishes that need cleaning visit them, just as a person who wants his hair cut goes to the barber. Other fishes recognise the barbers by sight and do not eat them.

Living together
Some fishes have a special relationship with another fish or animal. In general, the law of the sea is eat and be eaten. But some fishes seem to be safe, or immune, from much of the danger.

Commensalism
The word used to describe the sort of relationship there is between the remora and the shark, or the clownfish and the anemone is called 'commensalism'. Sometimes, a relationship between two animals is only good for one of the partners. The other may die as a result of it. This is called parasitism. The animal which uses the other is a parasite.

Enemies
Being a fish is a cut-throat life. There are many fishes ready to snap anything up given the slightest chance. So there is always a danger of being eaten. Most fishes are very wary of enemies. Few stay to fight.

Fighting
Some fishes, however, do fight. They are usually of the same species, and they do not fight to the death. These fights are about territory, which is the ground that 'belongs' to a fish, and in which he breeds. If another fish of the same species enters the territory then very likely a fight will break out. The owner of the territory usually wins.

The wild fighting fishes of Thailand fight each other over territory. They have been bred by the Thais both as aquarium fishes and as fighting fishes. In some parts of the world people place bets on the outcome of the fights. They are very beautiful fishes, but they are better kept apart.

The so-called kissing gourami is a freshwater fish from south-east Asia. It is a favourite aquarium fish, because when two fishes put their mouths together they look as if they are kissing. Actually, they are fighting each other.

Strange Friendships

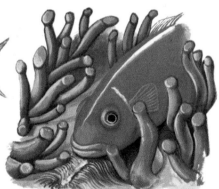

Pilot fishes swim near sharks and other large fishes. The legend is that they guide or pilot the sharks. The truth is less romantic. Pilot fishes get into the boundary layer of the shark. This is the layer of water round the shark's body which is moving with it. So the fish can travel as fast as the shark.

The clownfish lives on coral reefs. It uses a large sea anemone as a protector. Sea anemones have stinging cells in their tentacles to kill and eat other fishes. The clownfish is not hurt by these, but it lures other fishes into the anemone to be killed and eaten.

The wreckfish is often found swimming beside a piece of floating wreckage, or inside a floating box or barrel. It feeds on the barnacles that grow on the wreckage, but it also seems to treat the wreckage as a companion.

Strange Fishes

The waters of the earth contain many weird and wonderful creatures. Here are some of them.

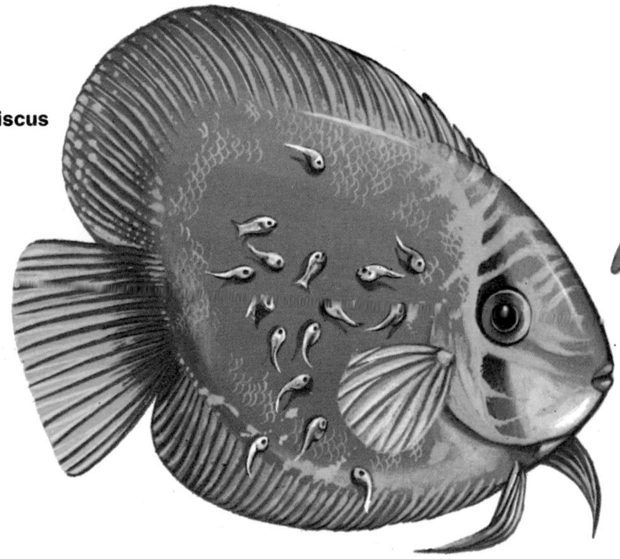

Discus

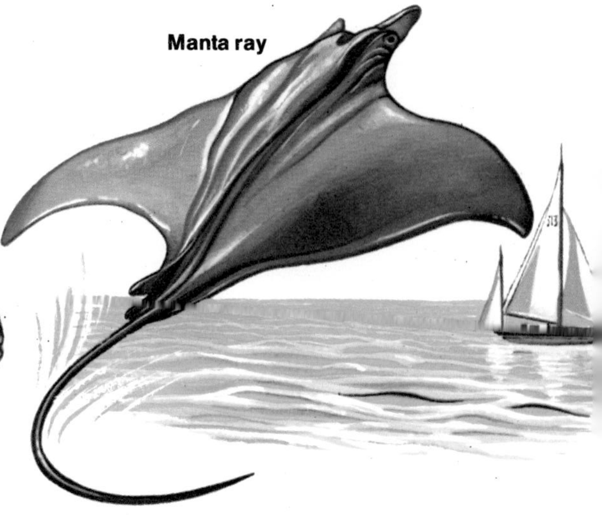

Manta ray

Hammerhead

Idiacanthus

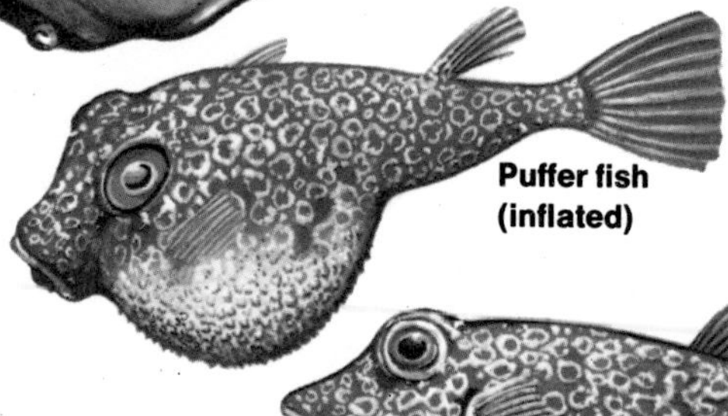

Puffer fish (inflated)

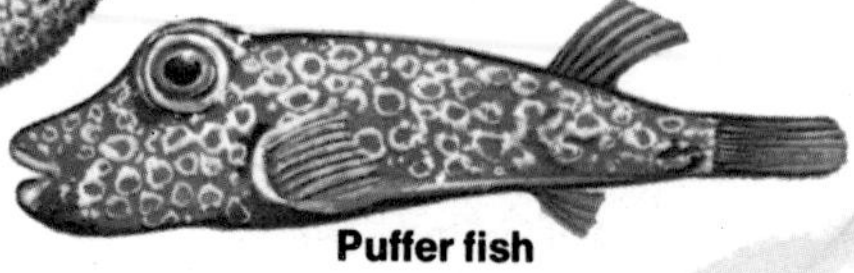

Puffer fish (deflated)

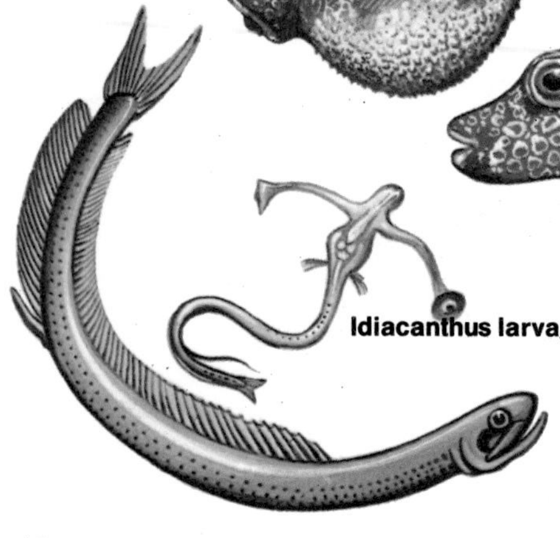

Idiacanthus larva

Rainbow parrotfish

Why Strange?

A thing is called strange when it is not the usual shape or colour, or when it behaves in an unusual way. The 'usual' sort of fish is one like the mackerel, with a 'fish-shaped' body and not very large fins.

Some Examples

The manta ray is strange because it is so big—20 feet (6 m.) across—and has a flattened body, like a skate. The discus fish also has a flattened body, but it is flattened from side to side. Its babies feed in a strange way, on the slime on the parent's body.

The hammerheaded shark has its eyes at each end of the 'hammerhead.' It is very grotesque.

Puffer fishes and porcupine fishes can blow themselves up so that their spines stand out. This makes it difficult for other fishes to swallow them. The strange thing about the idiacanthus is the difference in shape between the young and adult fish. The eyes of the young idiacanthus are out on stalks.

The rainbow parrotfish spins a sort of web, or 'nightgown' round itself when it settles down for the night. The archer fish can shoot down an insect with a stream of water drops from its mouth.

The scorpionfish has lots of long rays on its body, some of which are poisonous.

Living Fossils

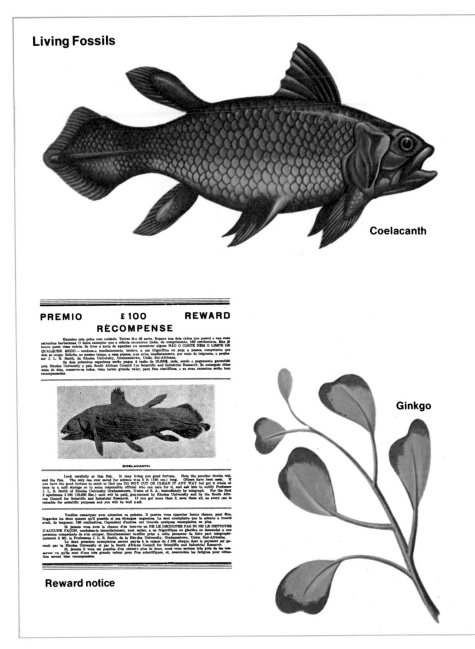

Coelacanth

Reward notice

Ginkgo

A fossil is the remains of something that lived long ago. A living fossil is different. Charles Darwin named a plant a living fossil. Its name is the ginkgo, and it is a tree found only in China and Japan. Millions of years ago, ginkgo trees were growing over most of the world. There were many different kinds. One by one these died out until only one was left. Even this was found in only a few places. It was all that was left of a widespread family.

There are a number of living fossils. The most famous is the coelacanth (seel-a-canth). It is a fish. About 90 million years or more ago, other fishes like the coelacanth lived in large numbers in rivers all over the world. Their fossils have been known for a long time, but nobody had ever seen one alive. The coelacanth family was thought to be extinct. Then, just before Christmas in 1938, a fishing boat put into East London, in South Africa, with its catch. Among the catch was a strange fish about three ft. (1 m.) long. It looked a little unusual, but Professor J. L. B. Smith, who studied fishes, knew at once it was a coelacanth. Professor Smith had notices printed (see left) promising a reward and he sent these round to fishermen. Then, just after Christmas Day, in 1952, he received news that another coelacanth had been caught off Madagascar, the large island to the east of South Africa. Since then a dozen or more have reached museums and laboratories. During the night of March 22-23, 1972, another coelacanth was caught and kept alive for a time off the Comoro Islands, west of Madagascar. Its colour was a brilliant blue. It was a female, weighing 22 lbs. (10 kg.), and was 35 ins. (889 mm.) long.

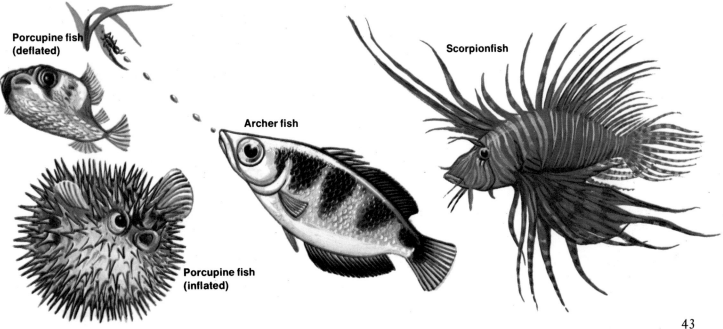

Porcupine fish (deflated)

Porcupine fish (inflated)

Archer fish

Scorpionfish

Man and the Sea

From time immemorial, man has relied on the rivers and the sea to feed him, and also to provide him with transport.

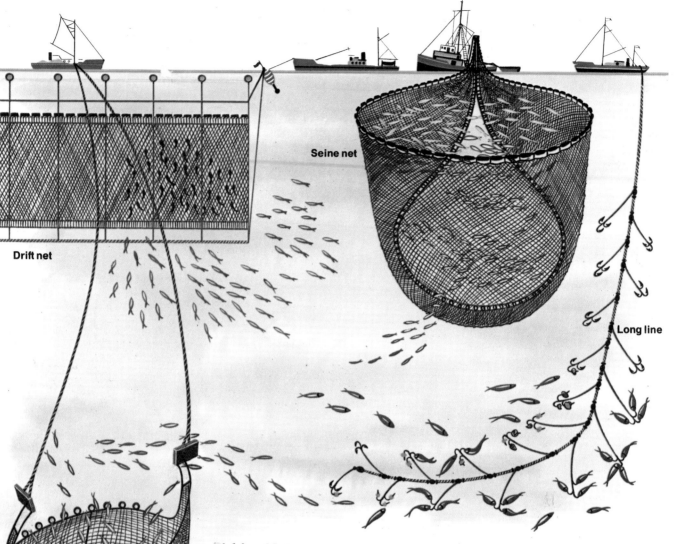

Seine net

Drift net

Long line

Otter trawl

Fishing Nets

Probably the first kind of net was the round cast net. This was thrown over a shoal of fishes. The early fishermen made nets that could be hauled along by boats so that they could take them to the fish instead of waiting for the fish to come to the nets. Today, three kinds of nets are used—the seine net, drift net and the otter trawl. The seine is a long net, buoyed up with floats, that is pulled out by a boat into a half-circle around a shoal of fish. The net is then pulled in, or towed, taking the fish with it.

The drift net is 160 ft. (50 m.) or so long and 40 ft. (12 m.) or more deep. It hangs like a curtain in the

sea, buoyed up by floats or corks. It catches fish that are near the bottom by day but come to the surface at night to feed.

The otter trawl is a large bag net about 100 ft. (30 m.) long with a wide mouth. Either side of the mouth is an 'otter board'. As the trawl is towed along the sea-bed the water pushes against the boards holding them apart, and keeps the mouth of the net open.

Long-line fishing means letting down a line which may be two miles (3 km.) long. It has shorter lines, known as snoods. Each snood has several hooks and there may be 500 hooks on a long line.

Anchovetas are small silvery fishes three to six ins. (70-150 mm.) long living in the Pacific Ocean, off the coast of South America. They swim about in huge shoals of countless thousands.

The anchoveta fishery is only about 20 years old. For a long time the anchovetas have been the food of sea birds that nested and roosted on islands off the coast of Peru. The birds' droppings accumulated on the islands forming a thick layer of guano. This is a wonderful fertilizer for the soil. The people of South America, of Peru especially, gathered the guano and exported it. Guano meant wealth for those who traded in it. Thousands of tons were exported each year. Birds must eat 20 tons of anchovetas to yield a ton of guano. Somebody had the idea of taking the fish direct, to turn it into fertilizer. Moreover, some could be eaten, some could be turned into fish meal for poultry and pigs and still there would be enough for fertilizer. A new fishing industry sprang up. Fishing fleets grew like magic. Villages became flourishing towns. Factories grew up around the towns. In 1964, 7 million tons of anchovetas were caught.

From Fish To . . .

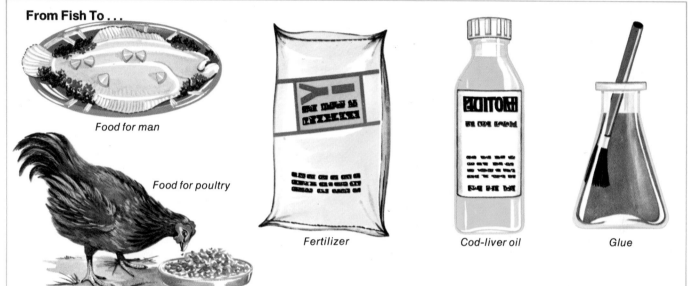

Food for man

Food for poultry

Fertilizer

Cod-liver oil

Glue

Fishes and Friends

Male

Female

The guppy feeds on mosquito larvae. Mosquitos spread the disease known as malaria. By eating the larvae, the guppies help to keep down malaria.

Crocodiles are fast disappearing. Their skins are used for making fancy leather. This is bad for the freshwater fisheries. The crocodiles eat the larger fishes that feed on the smaller food fishes.

The hippopotamus is becoming scarce. This is bad for the freshwater fisheries because hippo dung fertilizes the water, and produces food for the fishes.

Pollution

Rivers are often polluted by waste which is poured into them from factories. This has a harmful effect on river life.

Water

Natural waters contain a lot of oxygen, but they also contain small quantities of other chemicals. Fishes have been living in natural waters for millions of years. They are adapted to the waters and their slight impurities. The most important part of the water to a fish is the oxygen. It is as important to a fish as air is to humans, and for the same reason. Fishes, like land animals, need to breathe. Breathing means taking in oxygen.

Factory Waste

Waste from factories is often poured into rivers. This is the simplest way to get rid of it. But it is dangerous for life in the river. Some of the chemicals stay in the river. They are not carried away to the sea. In the end, the water becomes foul. Notice in the picture above how much life there is in the clean, natural water of the stream as it flows through the countryside. When it runs past factories, however, the water is dirty. It is black, with a scum on the surface. It has an unpleasant smell, and there is no life in it. It is polluted.

Oxygen

Oxygen taken from the water by fishes is replaced in two ways. Oxygen is dissolved into the water from the air at the surface. Water plants also produce oxygen when growing in sunshine. When the

water is murky, less sunshine reaches the plants. There is less oxygen for fishes to breathe. Poisonous chemicals kill off the plants, so there is even less oxygen. In the end, all life in the water dies.

Rainwater

Much of the water in a river comes from the ground. Rain and melting snow soak into the ground and drain into the river. Poisonous chemicals that kill weeds (called herbicides) or insects (insecticides) are washed into the ground by rain, and drain into the river with the water.

Starvation

Fishes must feed. Some eat small animals such as water fleas or insect larvae. These are the first to be killed off when a river becomes polluted. So pollution does not only mean a loss of oxygen for breathing, it means the fishes starve. In fact, everything starves, from the green plants to the larger fishes.

Ecology

The study of the dependence of plants on clean water and clean air, and of the dependence of animals on plants, and animals on each other is called ecology. Today, ecology is one of the most important sciences. Yet it is a very new science. The word ecology was used for the first time only 100 years ago.

One way to fight pollution is to find out whether water is polluted. The water can look clear yet contain a dangerous toxin. The only way to find out is to take some of the water and sample it. This means taking it to a laboratory for testing.

Sometimes pollution is detected when food is checked for poisons. This is always going on. There are scientists who spend all their time checking food to see that it is pure and clean.

The study of pollution is fairly new, and like all new sciences there are difficulties. For example, very little is known about what chemicals have always been in fishes' bodies, before the waters became polluted.

Recently, for example, it was found out that the sea fish, known as tuna, contained mercury. Mercury is a poisonous chemical which had somehow found its way into the sea, and therefore into the body of the tuna.

Scientists now believe this mercury level to be normal in tuna fishes.

These fishes have been killed by what is called toxic waste from factories. 'Toxic' is another word for poisonous. The word is used specially for the poisons that are there without anyone knowing it. If a fish could keep its mouth shut, it would be safe from toxic waste. But it must open its mouth to take in water for breathing. The toxins—or poisons—reach the gills. There they are taken into the blood and to all parts of the fish's body.

47

Myths and Legends

Sailors and travellers have always told wonderful tales about the sea. Many of these legends can perhaps be simply explained.

Drawings of sea serpents in old books show monsters that look like huge snakes attacking ships. These drawings were made by scholars who had heard the tales told by sailors.

There are stories of sea serpents with a line of fins running along the middle of the back. Tuna fishes sometimes swim in line with their back fins above the surface.

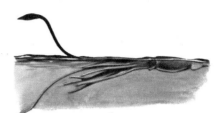

Squids have ten arms, eight short and two very long. Giant squids can be 60 ft. (18 m.) long. If one swam just under the surface and raised one of its long arms out of the water it would look like a huge snake.

The adult eel can grow to twelve times the length of its larva. Leptocephalus larvae six ft. (1.8 m.) long have been netted in deep water in various parts of the sea. Would they have grown to 72 ft. (22 m.)? And are there giant eels or some other giant fishes yet to be discovered?

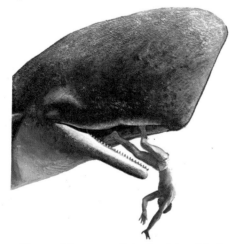

The most famous myth is about Jonah being swallowed by a leviathan, and then brought up again alive. Everyone thought the leviathan must have been a large whale, like the sperm whale.

Stories

Some stories are told which everyone knows are untrue. These are called myths. There are others, equally attractive, which are passed on by word of mouth from one generation to another, and these may or may not be true. These are called legends. There are myths and legends about the sea and its inhabitants.

One sea myth is about the mermaid. At one time this was a legend because many people believed it. Columbus, on his return from discovering America, noted in his log that he had seen mermaids there. They were manatees, sea animals something like dolphins. The females hold their babies to the breast to suckle them. So they looked human—at a distance.

Sea Serpents

The most widespread legend is about the sea serpent. Drawings in old books showed a huge snake attacking a ship.

A few scientists still believe in a sea serpent. They say that there are large animals in the sea about which people know very little. Therefore it is still possible there is a real sea serpent.

Nobody today really believes there are such things as mermaids. Yet a 17th century scientist claimed to have seen one. He described her even down to the shape of her finger nails, and he made a careful drawing of what she looked like. This drawing shows what most people think a mermaid looks like.

Facts and Figures

Largest sea fish
The whale shark measures 50 feet (15 m.) or more long. The basking shark and the great white shark both measure up to 40 feet (12 m.).

Largest man-eater shark
The great white shark may measure 33 feet (11 m.).

Largest river fish
The arapaima of tropical South America measures seven feet (2 m.) long, and weighs 246 lbs. (111 kg.). It is always said to grow to 15 feet (4.6 m.) in length, but this is a myth.

Smallest fish
The smallest fish is the Luzon goby, of the Philippines. It measures half-an-inch (12 mm.) long.

Longest-lived fish
A Russian sturgeon, or beluga, lived to be about 120 years old, and weighed over a ton.
Known ages of some other fishes are:

stickleback	five years
cod	20 years or more
plaice	60 years

Shortest-lived fish
There are 26 different kinds of annual fishes in the rivers of Africa and South America. They die at the end of the rainy season, when the rivers dry up. Before dying, they lay eggs that can withstand drying. These eggs hatch when the rainy season starts. So the fishes live much less than a year.

Greatest depth in the sea
35,802 feet (10,911 m.).

Deepest trench
The Mariana Trench in the Pacific is the deepest sea trench. It is 35,640 feet (10,863 m.) deep.

Fastest fish
The sailfish has been known to swim at a speed of 68 m.p.h. (109 k.p.h.).

Largest number of eggs
A ling 61 inches (1.5 m.) long, and weighing 54 lbs. (24 kg.) laid 28,361,000 eggs.

Most poisonous fish
Stonefishes of the Indian and Pacific Oceans are the most poisonous fishes. Their poison is extremely painful, and causes death within six hours. Luckily, not all such stings are fatal.

Most powerful electric discharge
Electric eel, with 550 volts.

Highest leap out of the water
A tarpon has been known to leap 18 feet (5 m.) high, and make a 30 feet (9 m.) arc.

Most ornamental fish
The turkeyfish is the most ornamental fish. It is also called the scorpionfish, lionfish, dragonfish, firefish, devilfish, zebrafish, featherfish, butterfly cod, and sausaulele.

Ugliest fish
This is very probably the stonefish.

Largest shoals
Herring are known to have as many as 3,000 million fishes in one shoal.

Longest name
The triggerfish is known in Hawaii as the humuhumu-nukunuku-apuaa.

Longest migration
European eels travel as much as 4,660 miles (7,500 km.) on a spawning migration from the Eastern Mediterranean or the Baltic. Quinnat salmon sometimes journey 2,250 miles (3,620 km.) up the Yukon river.

Speeds of fishes

	m.p.h.	k.p.h.
Bream	1.24	2
Chub	5	8
Stickleback	6.8	10.9
Tench	7	11.3
Eel	7.5	12
Carp	7.6	12.2
Mullet	8	12.9
Minnow	8.2	13.2
Dace	9.3	15
Roach	10	16.1
Perch	10.2	16.4
Barbel	11	17.7
Bass	12	19.3
Pike	20.5	32.9
Trout	23	37
Salmon	25	40.2
Blue shark	26.5	42.6
Tarpon	35	56.3
Flying fish	35	56.3
Tuna	44	70.8
Swordfish	60	96.6
Marlin	60	96.6
Sailfish	60	96.6

The difference in the shape of these fishes accounts for the difference in their speeds. Look back at some of the pictures of these fishes in the book. You will notice that the slower fishes like the carp and dace have fins halfway along their back. Faster fishes, like the pike and the sailfish (when moving), have fins that are set well back on the body. The shape is much more streamlined than that of the slower fishes. The sailfish, of course, tucks its big sail fin down when it wants to move fast.

Numbers of young born alive

Platys	10–75
Guppy	20–70
Tetras	100–150
Cichlids	150–350
Rosy barb	200–250
Blue gourami	250–950
Clown barb	3,000

Numbers of eggs laid
A 20 lb. (9 kg.) salmon laid 14,000 eggs. This is 600–700 eggs for each pound (0.45 kg.) of its body weight.
Other numbers are:

Haddock	250,000
Plaice	500,000
Sole	570,000
Flounder	1,000,000
Common carp	$2\frac{1}{2}$ million
Halibut	2,750,000
Cod	6,652,000
Turbot	9 million

World's catch of sea fish
40,000 million lbs. (18,144 million kg.) of fish are caught each year. This is only a small fraction, perhaps five per cent, of the total population of food fishes in the seas.

Fishing History
Many of the big sea ports on the North Sea began as herring fishing villages. Hamburg, in Germany, was founded in 809 A.D. as a herring port. This led to the Hanseatic League. For centuries this controlled the export trade of Europe.
In the 16th century, fishermen went across the Atlantic to Newfoundland. There, they started fishing for cod, with long lines. Cod led the English and the French to Canada, and cod became a source of wealth to the people of what is now the United States.

Swim-bladder gases
The gases in a fish's swim-bladder are the same as those in the air. But the proportions of the gases are different

Facts and Figures

in the swim-bladder. The gases are oxygen, carbon dioxide and nitrogen. There is more oxygen in the swim-bladder of a marine fish than in a freshwater fish. Deep-sea fishes sometimes have as much as 84 per cent oxygen in the swim-bladder. In fishes living deep in lakes, the amount of nitrogen can be as much as 94 per cent. Air is made up of 80 per cent nitrogen, less than one per cent carbon dioxide, and the rare gases, and the rest is made up of oxygen.

Rains of fishes
Rains of fishes have been reported in various parts of the world. The explanation seems to be that the fishes get carried up into the clouds by whirlwinds and waterspouts travelling across water.

In 1806 at Essen, in Germany, a large hailstone was found. Inside the hailstone was a carp $1\frac{1}{2}$ inches (38 mm.) long. Another fish fell from the sky at Jelapur, India, and weighed more than 6 lbs. (2.7 kg.).

Sharp sword
A swordfish is known to have gone through copper sheathing, then 4 inches (102 mm.) of board, then 12 inches (305 mm.) of solid white oak timber, $2\frac{1}{2}$ inches (63.5 mm.) of hard oak. The tip of its sword went through the head of a cask. This makes a total of $18\frac{1}{2}$ inches (469 mm.) of hard wood and metal.

Fish with the thickest skin
A large whale shark may have a skin four inches (102 mm.) or more thick.

Largest fish caught on rod and line
A great white shark was caught off South Australia in 1959, weighing 2,664 lbs. (1,208 kg.).

Heaviest known fish
A whale shark was estimated to weigh 90,000 lbs. (40,823 kg.). It was 59 ft. (18 m.) long.

Smallest marine fish
A goby living off the Marshall Islands in the South Pacific, is seldom more than $\frac{3}{5}$ in. (15 mm.) long.

Most ferocious freshwater fish
The piranha of South America has razor-sharp teeth. A shoal of piranhas are said to have eaten the flesh off a cow which had fallen into a river. It took only five minutes to pick the skeleton clean.

Most ferocious marine fish
The bluefish of the warmer parts of the Atlantic has been described as a living chopping machine. There are possibly 1,000,000,000 bluefish in the seas off the Atlantic coast of the United States. Each fish eats about ten other fishes each day, so, 10,000,000,000 fishes are eaten each day. Also, bluefish kill more fishes than they can eat. A shoal of them attacking a shoal of herrings or mackerels, leave a trail of bits of fish. A fish too large to be swallowed whole is bitten in two, one piece floating away. Bluefish probably kill over 2,000,000,000,000 other fishes (many of them about their own size or larger) in a year. Most bluefish weigh 3–5 lbs. (1–2 kg.), but the largest are 30 lbs. (14 kg.), and they may be up to two feet (610 mm.) long. Sometimes a shoal of bluefish will drive a shoal of horse mackerel on to a beach where they become piled up in rows.

Greatest depth from which a fish has been brought to the surface (in a net)
A fish has been brought to the surface from a depth of 23,392 ft. (7,129 m.), in the Sunda Trench, south of Java, in 1951.

Greatest depth at which fishes are known to live
The greatest depth at which it is known for certain that fishes are living is in the Puerto Rico Trench in the Caribbean Sea, at a depth of 26,132 feet (7,965 m.).

Numbers of gills in sharks
All sharks have five gill-slits, except the griset, or six-gilled shark, and the frilled shark, both of which have six. The perlon has seven gill-slits, and is often called the seven-gilled shark.

Facts about breathing
Water is made up of one part of oxygen to two of hydrogen. Water exposed to air takes in more oxygen. This oxygen is passed on through water, and can go right down to the deepest seas. A fish uses this extra oxygen for breathing.

A man takes 20–25 breaths a minute. In fishes the rate may be as low as 12 breaths per minute (in a wrasse) to 150 (in a minnow).

The rate of breathing differs because some fishes need more oxygen than others. A trout must have at least three to five parts of oxygen per million of its body weight. A carp can live with less than 3.5 parts per million. So trout live in swiftly flowing streams, because water in movement takes in much more oxygen. A carp can live in a small, muddy pond.

The colder the water, the more oxygen it can hold. So trout live best in cold streams. Also, fishes are much more abundant in cold seas. Polar seas are noted for the large numbers of fishes living in them.

Glossary

Aestivate:
to be sleepy, or to go to sleep, during a hot season or a long drought.

Aggression:
the act of showing fight or of showing signs of being about to attack. It is used especially of the animal or person who starts the fight or quarrel.

Bony fish:
a fish with a skeleton of bone, in contrast to a cartilaginous fish.

Breeding migration:
when an animal feeds in one place and then moves to another to breed.

Breeding season:
this is the time during which an animal chooses a mate and brings up a family, even if that family is no more than one young one. Some animals have several families in one season.

Buoyancy:
the power of floating.

Camouflage:
disguising something by means of colour.

Carnivore:
a word that has two meanings. It can mean any animal that eats meat, or it can be taken to mean any animal, like cats and dogs, that is a flesh-eater and that eats mainly meat.

Cartilaginous fish:
a fish that has a skeleton made entirely of cartilage or gristle, such as sharks. Other fishes have skeletons of bone.

Chromatophore:
(kro-mat-o-for) a cell or group of cells in the skin that contain pigments. The cells can change their shape and in so doing alter the colour of an animal.

Commensalism:
a partnership between two animals, two plants, or a plant and an animal in which food is shared.

Cryptic:
from a Greek word meaning 'hidden'. It is used for an animal with dull colours that make it almost impossible to see against its natural background. The word has a similar meaning to camouflage, but cryptic colours are more broken up.

Current:
a mass of water or air moving in one direction.

Ecology:
the part of biology that deals with the relationship of an animal with its environment.

Embryo:
a young plant or animal in the early stages of development, before its body is properly formed.

Environment:
everything in its surroundings that affects a plant or animal.

Extinct:
when the last member of a species dies, the species becomes extinct.

Fertilization:
when a sperm (short for spermatozoon) or male sex cell enters an ovum, which is the female sex cell, the ovum becomes fertilized. A fertilized ovum grows into a baby.

Fin:
a fold of skin supported by rods or rays, used by fishes in swimming.

Fish:
a cold-blooded vertebrate (an animal with a backbone) that lives all or most of its life in water. It breathes by gills only, or by gills mainly, even when it has lungs, and it has a scaly skin.

Food chain:
a sequence of plants or animals in which each one is the food of another one in the sequence.

Fry:
young fishes soon after they hatch.

Gill:
a breathing organ in which the blood flows through blood vessels that lie just under a thin layer of skin. The oxygen is taken up from the surrounding water, and waste substances, like carbon dioxide, are given out to the water.

Gill cover:
a thin plate of bone which forms a lid over the gill chamber. It protects the delicate gills inside. Its scientific name is operculum.

Habitat:
the place, or the environment in which a plant or animal lives.

Herbivore:
an animal that eats nothing but plant food, or mainly plant food.

Larva:
an embryo that is able to live on its own before it has grown to be like its parents, or to look like them.

Lateral line:
a line of scales on each side of a fish's body running from just behind the head to the tail-fin. Each scale covers a small sense organ that can detect vibrations in the water.

Living fossil:
a plant or animal belonging to a species that is still living. Most of its near relatives, however, have become extinct.

Milt:
the fluid given out by a male fish at spawning time. This fluid contains the spermatozoa, or male sex cells.

Mucus:
a slime given out by special cells in the skin.

Natural selection:
Nature's way of selecting the best to be the parents of the next generation. Animals and plants less able to survive than others, either because they are weak or not adapted to their environment, are killed off.

Notochord:
a stiff rod that appears in the embryo, around which the backbone is laid down.

Operculum:
another name for the gill cover. It is also the name used for other plant or animal lids.

Ovipositor:
a special tube in female insects and fishes. Eggs are laid through the tube into places where they will be protected.

Plankton:
small plants and animals, mostly of microscopic size. They live in water and cannot swim against a current. They must drift with it.

Scale:
a small flat plate in an animal's skin that may be bony or horny. It helps to protect the skin.

Scavenger:
an animal that feeds on pieces of dead plant or animal and in doing so helps to keep its environment clean.

Sense organ:
an organ containing one of the senses, such as the eye for seeing, the nose for smelling, ears for hearing, or tongue for tasting. Some sense organs are very small and are made up of sense cells scattered over the skin, like the sense of touch.

Spawn:
to lay eggs in water.

Spermatozoa:
the male sex cells. One cell is called a spermatozoon, or sperm for short. The plural of spermatozoon is spermatozoa.

Swim-bladder:
a long silvery bag lying below the backbone of a fish, seen when a fish is cut open to be cooked. In a live fish it is filled with air or some other gas and acts as a float. It gives the fish buoyancy.

Territory:
an area of land or a volume of water occupied by an animal, or a pair or a group of animals. The territory is large enough to give them the food they need.

Vortex:
a spiral movement or swirling mass of water forming a whirlpool, like the Sargasso Sea.

Distribution of Fishes

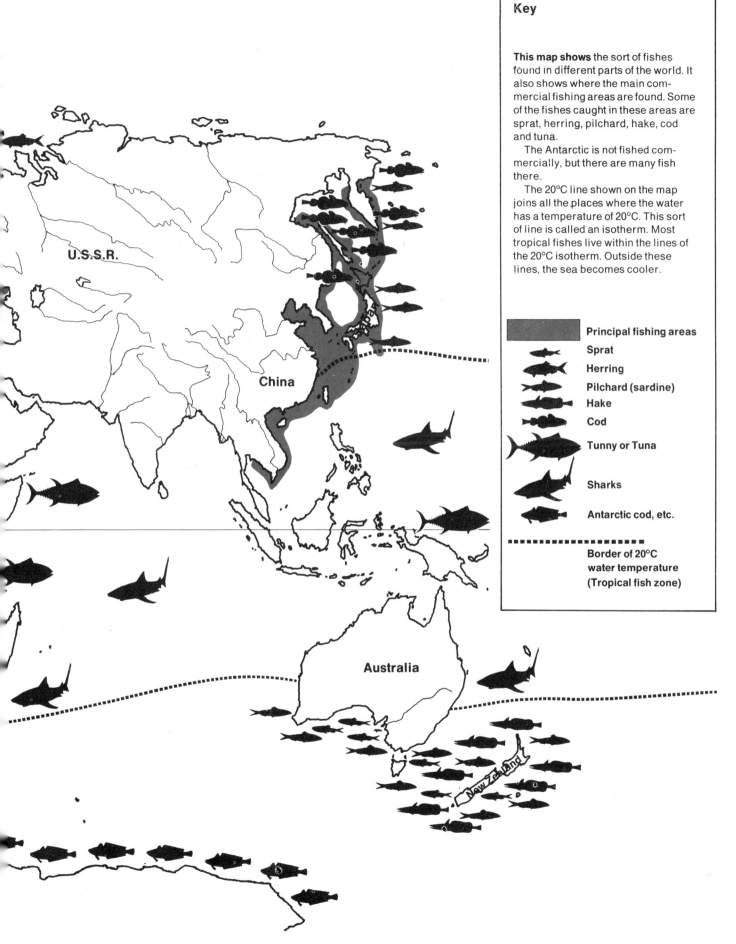

U.S.S.R.

China

Australia

New Zealand

53

Keeping Goldfish

For metric conversions of the measurements used here, please turn to the table on page 61.

Goldfish are a domesticated form of the wild goldfish, a kind of carp native to China. They were first cultivated by the Chinese in 960 A.D., who kept them in earthenware bowls. In 1500 A.D. they were taken to Japan. The Japanese have developed most of the present varieties.

Five of the main types are shown here—the common goldfish, fantail, veiltail, comet and lionhead. The shubunkin is also a popular type of goldfish.

Goldfish are often kept in glass bowls. Sometimes they live up to ten years even in a bowl. Usually they do not. A goldfish is better kept in an aquarium. A glass bowl is too much like a prison for the fish.

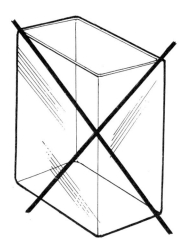

A tall glass container should not be used. A fish needs oxygen. The oxygen in water is dissolved at the surface, from the air. If the surface of water in contact with the air is small, it will not contain much oxygen.

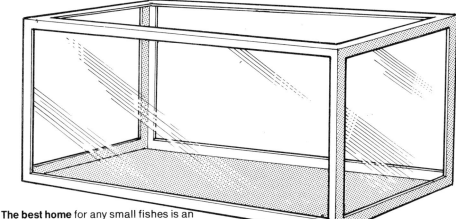

The best home for any small fishes is an aquarium with a metal frame that will not rust, and with glass sides.

Surface Area

The water in an aquarium must have a large surface area. To find the surface area, multiply the length of the tank by the width. If the tank is 24 inches long by 12 inches wide, the surface area is $24 \times 12 = 288$ square inches. Each fish must have 20 square inches of surface for every inch of its body length, excluding the tail. So, divide 288 by 20 to find out how many fishes can be kept. This gives just over 14. So you can have 14 fishes one inch long, seven two-inch fishes, four three-inch fishes, or three four-inch fishes. Do not overcrowd the aquarium,

or the fishes may die.

Do not put shells in for decoration. They may be dissolved slightly, and this is bad for the fishes. Always wash sands and plants before putting them in the water. Keep the water clean by taking out uneaten food, dead plants or dead fish. Keep the temperature around 15°C (60°F). Never make the temperature change too quickly.

Never put an aquarium on a sunny window-sill. Too much light causes a green coating on the inside of its walls. This is a layer of very small algae. If it happens, shade the aquarium. The algae will disappear.

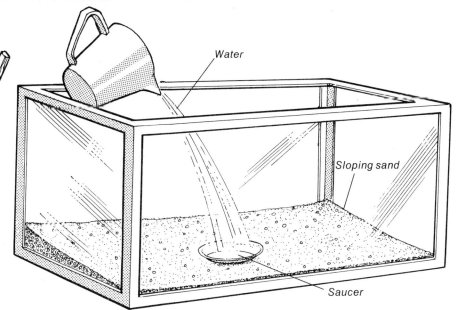

Stir the sand thoroughly

Wait until water is clear

Water

Sloping sand

Saucer

Sand should be put at the bottom of the aquarium. This must be well-washed. Put it in a bucket under a running tap, and stir it all the time. When the water from it runs clear, the sand is clean. Do not use gravel or white sand. Gravel traps dirt. White sand makes some fishes go pale.

The sand should slope from the back of the tank to the front. Make it about two inches high at the back, sloping down to one inch at the front. Refuse, such as stale, uneaten food, will all collect at the front of the slope, where you can see it and remove it easily.

Fill the tank by pouring water gently onto a saucer on the sand. This way, the sand will not be disturbed and make the water cloudy. Use rainwater if possible. If you use tap water, leave it to stand a few days before filling the tank.

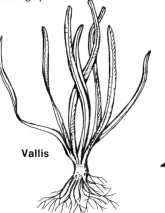

Vallis

Sagittaria

Myriophyllum

Canadian Waterweed

Cabomba

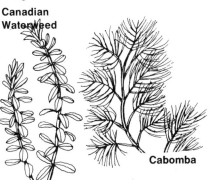

Fishes need oxygen for breathing. Oxygen is part of the mixture of gases called air. It dissolves from the air at the water surface. Plants give out oxygen during the day, and take in carbon dioxide. At night they do the opposite. It has always been thought that the

oxygen that water plants give out by day helps animals. Now it is found that they take in almost as much oxygen at night as they give out by day. So plants are not needed in aquaria to help fishes breathe. Many fishes, however, like to swim or hide among plants.

More important, goldfish like to eat them. Some of the best and cheapest plants are valisneria (often called vallis), sagittaria, myriophyllum, cabomba and Canadian waterweed. The last two need not be planted in the sand, as they grow well just floating.

Feeding

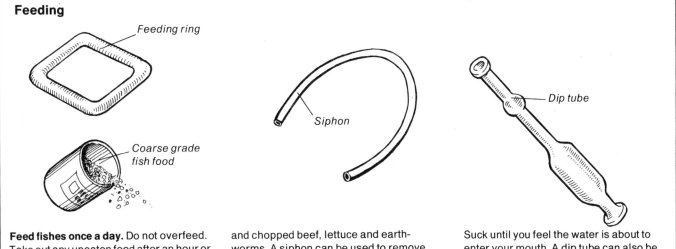

Feeding ring

Coarse grade fish food

Siphon

Dip tube

Feed fishes once a day. Do not overfeed. Take out any uneaten food after an hour or so, or it will poison the water as it decays. Give coarse grade food from pet shops,

and chopped beef, lettuce and earthworms. A siphon can be used to remove refuse or to empty the tank. Use a piece of rubber tubing. Put one end in the water.

Suck until you feel the water is about to enter your mouth. A dip tube can also be used to take uneaten food from the water. It can be bought at a pet shop.

Checking Pollution

Rain, snow, hail, etc., drains through soil into rivers

Transpiration

Rain, snow, hail, etc., falling direct onto water

Evaporation

Water is always on the move. People use it. It evaporates, which means the sun's heat draws it up into the atmosphere and makes it 'disappear'. Plants take water from the soil and lose it through their leaves to the atmosphere. This is called transpiration. The water removed in these ways is replaced by frost, dew, rain, hail, snow and ice. So water goes through a sort of circular movement, called a cycle. It is known as a hydrological cycle. 'Hydro' comes from the Greek word for water.

Sun

Water surface

When animals breathe out they give off carbon dioxide, which plants take in. Their dead bodies rot away and produce salts on which plants feed.

Water plant

Plants use energy from the sun and carbon dioxide from water. They give off oxygen during the day. Animals breathe it in. They are also a source of food for animals.

Fish

Plants and animals and the water in which they live make up a balanced community, or ecosystem. So long as the balance is maintained, everything flourishes. During the day, plants take in carbon dioxide which animals breathe out; they give off oxygen which animals breathe in. At night, plants give out carbon dioxide and take in oxygen.

Fishes rest then, so they need less oxygen, leaving more for the plants.

Some animals eat the plants. Other animals eat the plant-eating animals. When plants and animals die their bodies rot, or decompose. They become broken down to produce salts, such as nitrates. Plants take in these salts for food.

'Pure' water contains many substances it collects from decaying plants and animals, from the soil it drains through, from the air, and from breathing plants and animals. Some of these substances are carbon, nitrogen, hydrogen, sulphur and phosphorus. Some of them could be harmful in large quantities. The oxygen breaks them down into carbon dioxide, water, and salts called nutrients. They are then harmless and can also be used by living things. Oxygen is therefore very important. It comes mainly from the air. Some comes from plants. If the amount of other substances in the water is too great, then all the oxygen gets used up before it can be replaced, and pollution happens. Sometimes this pollution happens naturally, as in stagnant pools. Sometimes, man-made pesticides and detergents contain poisonous substances. If they are poured into the river in great quantities, then the oxygen cannot cope, and the water becomes polluted.

All life depends on the sun. Plants need the sun's energy to make their food. The sun gives warmth. Water is transparent so light can travel through it to the plants.

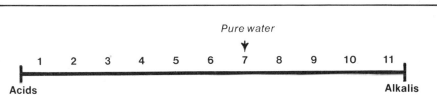

Pure water

```
     1   2   3   4   5   6   7   8   9   10   11
```
Acids   Alkalis

Badly-polluted water looks dead; it has no sparkle. Sometimes the bad smell of the water will tell you that it is polluted. Best of all, your eyes will be a guide. If there are water fleas, freshwater shrimps or insect larvae in the water, it is likely to be pure enough to drink. If there is a frog in the water it will be pure. On the other hand, rat-tailed maggots, which are larvae of hoverflies, only breathe air through their telescopic 'tail' and they live in foul water. Some water may be so far gone it has no animal life in it. There may be a factory or sewage polluting it.

Today, water can be easily and more thoroughly tested by using a Universal Indicator Paper. This paper changes colour in water, depending on what substances are present. If there are acids in the water, the paper turns red. If there are alkalis in the water, the paper turns blue. The exact shade the paper turns will show the pH value of the water. The letters pH are used with a scale of colours numbered from one to eleven, to measure the strength of acids and alkalis. Pure, clean water should be neutral. This means it should have a pH value of about seven, and be neither acid nor alkaline.

If the water is chalky, the pH will be nearer eight or nine because the water is slightly alkaline. If the water comes from a peaty pool it is acid, and the pH will be five or lower. On a sunny summer day, the pH of pond water could be as high as nine. This is because the sun helps plants to take in more carbon dioxide from the water. This makes the water less acid, so the pH value is higher.

Books of 20 leaves of Universal Indicator Paper, together with a colour coding chart from one to eleven, cost 5p each, and can be obtained from A. N. Beck and Sons Scientific, 147 High Road, South Tottenham, London N15 6DQ.

If you use Universal Indicator Paper and also check on the water life you will be able to tell whether the water is polluted or not.

Water

A puddle of water dries up and disappears in the sun. The water has evaporated. Evaporation is taking place all the time on the surfaces of the waters of the earth. Also, trees and plants take moisture from the soil through their roots, and lose it to the atmosphere through their leaves. The water that is being taken away is replaced by rain, hail, dew, frost, ice and snow.

Water has always been important to man, as well as to plants and animals. Man cannot live very long without pure water to drink. Cities were often situated on or near a river. Its water provided not only water to drink, and for the crops, but also a means of transport.

Water must be clean and oxygen-filled to support life. Water which is dirty, or polluted, and has no oxygen in it, is of no use to anyone. There has always been some pollution, but if it is natural it is readily put right. The damaging pollution today has been caused by discharging chemicals, pesticides, detergents and untreated sewage into rivers and streams. They use up all the oxygen, which is trying to break them down and make them harmless, so the water turns foul and all life in it dies.

It is important to our very life on earth that our sources of water do not get polluted.

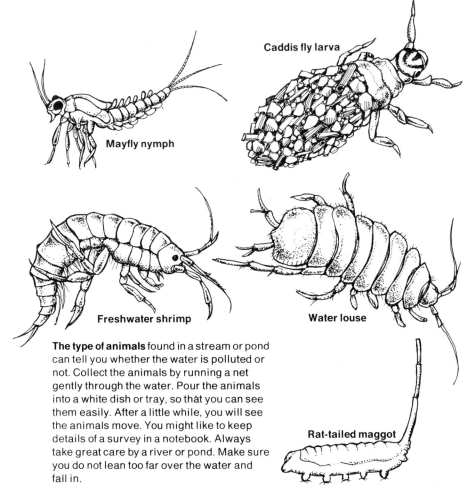

Caddis fly larva

Mayfly nymph

Freshwater shrimp

Water louse

Rat-tailed maggot

The type of animals found in a stream or pond can tell you whether the water is polluted or not. Collect the animals by running a net gently through the water. Pour the animals into a white dish or tray, so that you can see them easily. After a little while, you will see the animals move. You might like to keep details of a survey in a notebook. Always take great care by a river or pond. Make sure you do not lean too far over the water and fall in.

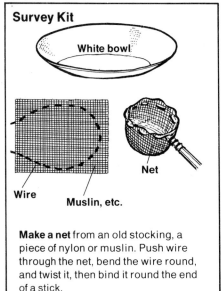

Survey Kit

White bowl

Wire   Muslin, etc.   Net

Make a net from an old stocking, a piece of nylon or muslin. Push wire through the net, bend the wire round, and twist it, then bind it round the end of a stick.

How to Draw Fishes

Basic Shape

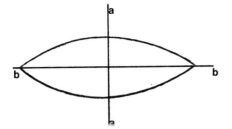

Begin with a cross (aa) and (bb). Draw two curves, one on top and one below the horizontal line.

Position of Fins

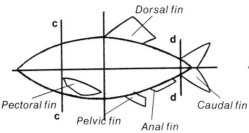

Add another vertical line (cc) on the left-hand side of line (aa) about half-way along Draw another line (dd) near the end of the curves. Fit the fins in using these lines as guides.

Eye, Mouth and Gill Cover

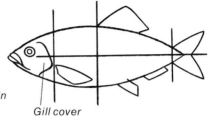

Fit in the eye (two circles, one inside the other), the mouth (bottom lip farther forward than top lip), and the gill cover.

Pattern of Scales

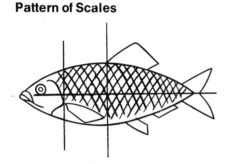

Draw criss-cross lines on the body of the fish. Use them as guides for the pattern of the scales. Round off each 'diamond' shape at one end as shown.

Finished Fish

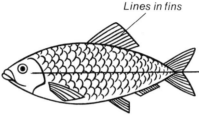

Round off all 'diamonds' to give correct scale shape. Put in some lines on the fins.

Scales

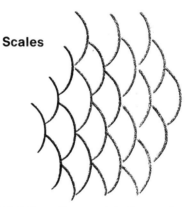

This is the pattern made by the overlapping scales that many fishes have.

Fins

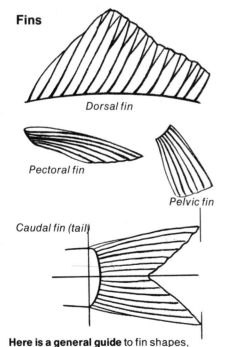

Here is a general guide to fin shapes, looked at from the side.

Eye

Head-on View

Top: The eye of a fish has a rounded pupil.
Below: How to draw a head-on view of a fish. Notice the gill covers and protruding eyes.

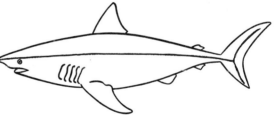

The shark has very small scales, called denticles. They cannot be seen on a drawing like the one above. It does not have gill covers, so five naked gills can be seen. It does not have veined fins like a bony fish.

The fins are supported by fin rays, like those of bony fishes, but the skin covering them is thicker so they cannot easily be seen.

Another difference from bony fishes is in the tail. Instead of having upper and lower halves (called lobes), each more or less equal, the upper lobe of a shark's tail is much larger than the lower lobe.

Names and Orders

The Animal Kingdom

The animal kingdom has been classified by scientists into groups of related animals.

Originally, people referred to animals just by using the word 'fish' or 'dog'. They would describe a particular fish by saying it was, for example, a jawless fish. Gradually, as more and more animals were discovered and studied by scientists, the animals were grouped in special ways.

Linnaeus

A Swedish scientist called Carl Linnaeus who lived in the 18th century, wrote a book in which he classified animals, grouping them in different ways. He chose the two languages which all scholars spoke all over the world. These languages were Latin and Greek. He even changed his name to Carolus Linnaeus, which is the Latin form of the name.

He introduced a system of giving each species two names, one for the genus and one for the species.

Fishes

There are basically three main types of fishes. Some are jawless, others are cartilaginous, which means their skeletons are made from gristle instead of bone, and the third type are fishes with bony skeletons, called bony fishes.

These three types make up the three main classes in the classification of fishes. All fishes fall into one or the other of these classes. The classes are divided again into sub-classes, and orders.

International

In this way, scientists from different countries, all speaking different languages, know exactly what fish they are talking about. They refer to the fish by its Latin or Greek name.

The list below shows how many types of fishes there are.

PHYLUM Chordata
(Animals with a notochord)
SUB-PHYLUM Vertebrata
(Animals with backbones)
CLASS Agnatha
(Jawless fishes)
Order Petromyzoniformes
(Lampreys)
Order Myxiniformes
(Hagfishes)
CLASS Chondrichthyes
(Cartilaginous fishes)
Order Hexanchiformes
(Frilled sharks)
Order Heterodontiformes
(Primitive sharks)
Order Lamniformes
(Modern sharks)
Order Rajiformes
(Skates and rays)
INFRACLASS Holocephali
Order Chimaeriformes
(Chimaeras or rabbitfishes)
CLASS Teleostomi
(Bony fishes)
SUB-CLASS Osteichthyes or Pisces
(Bony fishes)
Order Acipenseriformes
(Sturgeon)
Order Polypteriformes
(Bichir)
Order Amiiformes
(Bowfin)
Order Semionotiformes
(Gars or garpikes)
Division Teleostei
Order Elopiformes
(Tarpons)
Order Anguilliformes
(Eels)
Order Clupeiformes
(Herrings)
Order Osteoglossiformes
(Bonytongues)
Order Salmoniformes
(Salmon, trout)
Order Gonorhynchiformes
(Sand-fishes)
Super-order Ostariophysi
Order Cypriniformes
(Carps)

Order Siluriformes
(Catfishes)
Order Myctophiformes
(Lantern fishes)
Order Polymixiiformes
(no common name)
Order Percopsiformes
(Trout-perch)
Order Batrachoidiformes
(Toadfishes)
Order Indostomiformes
(no common name)
Order Gobiesociformes
(Clingfishes)
Order Lophiiformes
(Anglerfishes)
Order Gadiformes
(Cods)
Order Atheriniformes
(Sand smelts, flying fishes
and toothcarps)
Order Lampridiformes
(Moonfish, dealfishes)
Order Beryciformes
(Squirrel- or soldier-fishes)
Order Zeiformes
(John Dory)
Order Gasterosteiformes
(Sticklebacks, pipefishes
and seahorses)
Order Channiformes
(Snakeheads)
Order Synbranchiformes
(Cuchia)
Order Scorpaeniformes
(Scorpionfishes and gurnards)
Order Dactylopteriformes
(Flying gurnard)
Order Pegasiformes
(Dragon fishes)
Order Perciformes
(Perches)
Order Pleuronectiformes
(Plaice and other flatfishes)
Order Tetraodontiformes
(Boxfishes, trunkfishes)
INFRACLASS Crossopterygii
Order Holoptychiiformes
(Lobe-finned fishes)
Order Coelacanthiformes
(Coelacanth)
INFRACLASS Dipnoi
(Lungfishes)
Order Ceratodontiformes
(Lungfishes)

Index to Pictures and Text

Numbers in bold type refer to illustrations.

Alevin, 33, **33**
Anableps, 23, **23**
Anchoveta, 45, **45**
Anchovy, **24**
Angelfish, 18, **18, 37**
   Emperor angelfish, **37**
   French angelfish, **37**
   Koran angelfish, **37**
Anglerfish, 35, **35,** 59
Annual fish, 30, 49
Aquarium, 36, 41, 54–55
Arapaima, 49
Archer fish, **42, 43**
Barbel, 49
Barber fish, 40, **40**
Basking shark, 17, **17**
Barracuda, 24
Bass, 49
Beluga, 49
Bichir, 31, **31,** 59
Bitterling, 29, **29**
Black clownfish, 37
Bluefish, 50
Bone, 8
Bony fish, 17, 23, 31, 50, 59
Bonytongue, 59
Bowfin, 59
Boxfish, 59
Bream, 49
Breeding migration, 50
Breeding season, 26, 29, 50
Bullhead, **13**
Butterfish, 29, **29**
Butterfly fish, 18, **18**
Camouflage, 20–21, 50
   Cryptic camouflage, 21
Carbon dioxide, 50, 55, 57
Carp, **13,** 30–31, **31,** 49–50, 59
Carpet shark, 20, **20**
Cartilage, 8, 23
Cartilaginous fish, 17, 50, 59
Catfish, 15, **15,** 17, **17,** 23, **23,** 31, 59
   Electric catfish, **38**
   Glass catfish, **36**
Cephalaspis, 8, **8**
Chimaera, **38,** 59
Chlorophyll, 24
Chromatophore, 19, **19,** 51
Chub, 49
Cichlid, 29, **29,** 49
   Velvet cichlid, 27, **27**
Climbing perch, 17, **17**
Clingfish, 59
Clown barb, 49
Clownfish, **37,** 40–41, **41**

Cod, 30, **30,** 49–50, 53, 59
Cod-liver oil, 45, **45**
Coelacanth, 43, **43,** 59
Commensalism, 40, 51
Copepod, 30
Coral reef, 12, 36, 41
Courting, courtship, 26, 29
Crocodile, 45, **45**
Crustacean, **25**
Cryptic camouflage, 21, 51
Ctenoid scale, 31, **31**
Cuckoo wrasse, 19, **19**
Cycloid scale, 31, **31**
Dace, **13,** 49
Deciduous scale, 31
Denticle, 31, **31**
Diatom, 30
Dinichthys, 9, **9**
Discus fish, 42, **42**
Dogfish, 28, **28**
Dragon fish, 59
Drift net, 44, **44**
Drumfish, 39, **39**
Ecology, 47, 51
Eel, 13, **13,** 30–32, **32,** 48–49, **48,** 59
   Conger eel, 31
   Eel egg, 32
   Eel fare, 32
   Electric eel, 38, 49
   Glass eel (elver, young eel),
   30, **30,** 32, **32**
   Gulper eel, 35, **35**
   Leptocephalus (eel larva), 30, **30,**
   32, **32,** 48
   Silver eel, 32
Egg, 26–30, **30,** 32, 49
Elver (glass eel, young eel), 30, **30,**
   32, **32**
Fertilization, 29, 51
Fertilizer, 45, **45**
Fighting fish, 29, **29,** 36, **36,** 41, **41**
File fish, 20, **20**
Fin, 23, 26–27, 30–31, 39, 42
Fingerling, 33, **33**
Fish
   Body, 22–23
   Breathing, 16–17, 50
   Definition, 51
   Distribution, 52–53
   Food, 24–25
   How born, 28–29
   How to draw, 58
   Mating and breeding, 26–27
   Myths and legends, 48
Fishing, 44
Flatfish, 18–19, **19,** 59
Flounder, 19, **19,** 49
Flying fish, 12, **12,** 39, **39,** 49

Food chain, 24–25, **24–25,** 51
Food pyramid, 24–25, **24–25**
Fossil, 8, 10–11, **10,** 31, 43
   Living fossil, 43
Frog, 8, **13, 25**
Frogfish, 12
Fry, 29–30, **30,** 33, **33,** 51
Ganoid scale, 31, **31**
Garfish, **24,** 39
Gill, 16–17, **16,** 47, 51
   Gill cover, 16–17, 39, 51
Gingko, 43, **43**
Goby, 50
Goldfish, 17, **17,** 54–55, **54**
Gourami,
   Blue gourami, 49
   Kissing gourami, 41, **41**
Griset, 50
Gristle, 8, 23
Guano, 45
Gudgeon, **13**
Gulf Stream, 21
Gunnel, 29, **29**
Guppy, 36, **36,** 45, **45,** 49
Gurnard, **12,** 59
Habitat, 12, 21, 51
Haddock, 49
Hagfish, 8, 40, **40,** 59
Hake, 53
Halibut, 49
Hammerhead shark, 42, **42**
Hanseatic League, 49
Hatchet fish, 35, **35**
Herbicide, 47
Herring, **12, 24,** 25, 30–31, 49, 59
   Geographical distribution, 12, 53
Hippopotamus, 45, **45**
Idiacanthus, 42, **42**
Insect, 13, 17, 47
Insecticide, 47
Invertebrate, 9
Ipnops, 35, **35**
Iridocyte, 18–19
Jamoytius, 8, **8**
Jawless fish, 59
Jellyfish, 8, **9**
Jigsaw triggerfish, **37**
John Dory, 59
Kelp (seaweed) 12, **12**
Lamprey, 8, 27, **27,** 59
Lantern fish, 34–35, **35,** 59
Larva, 29–30, **30,** 32, **42,** 51
Lateral line, 23, **23,** 31, 51
Leaffish, 20, **20**
Leptocephalus, 30, **30,** 32, **32,** 48
Ling, 30, 49
Linnaeus, 59
Living fossil, 43, 51

Long line, 44, **44,** 50
Lungfish, 17, **17,** 59
Luzon goby, 49
Lyretail molly, **36**
Mackerel, 12, **12, 24,**25, 42
Mahseer, 31
Malaria, 45
Mallard, **13**
Manatee, 48
Marianas Trench, 34, 49, 50
Marlin, 49
Mass death, 11
Mating, 29
Mating season, 26
Mercury, 47
Mermaid, 48, **48**
Mermaid's purse, 28, **28**
Migration, 32–33, 49–50
Milt, 27, 29, 51
Minnow, 13, 49, 50
Molly, **36**
Moorish idol, **37**
Mosquito, 45
Mudskipper, 17, **17**
Mullet, 49
Mussel, **9,** 29, **29**
Natural selection, 51
Nest, 26–27
Nets, 44, **44**
Nitrogen, 50
Nostril, 17
Notochord, 51, 59
Ocean sunfish, 12, **12,** 39, **39,** 59
Operculum, 51
    See also Gill cover
Opisthoproctus, 35, **35**
Osteolepis, 8, **8**
Otter trawl, 44, **44**
Ovipositor, 29, **29,** 51
Oxygen, 16–17, 22, 46–47, 50, 55–56
Paleontologist, 10
Parasite, parasitism, 40
Parr mark, 33, **33**
Parrot fish, 12, **12**
    Rainbow parrotfish, 42, **42**
Perch, 13, **25,** 31, **31,** 49, 59
    Climbing perch, 17, **17**
Perlon, 50
Picasso fish, **37**
Piccard, Dr. J., 50
Pike, **13,** 25, **25,** 30, 49
Pilchard, 25, 31, 53
    See also Sardine
Pilot fish, 41, **41**
Pipefish, **24,** 28, **28,** 59
    Banded pipefish, **37**
Piranha, 50
Placoid scale, 31, **31**
Plaice, 12, 22, 30–31, **30,** 49, 59
Plankton, 16, 51
    Animal plankton, **24,** 25
    Plant plankton, 11, **24–25,** 25
Platys, 49

Poison, 19–21, 38, 47, 49
Pollution, 46–47, 56
    Checking pollution, 56–57
Porcupine fish, 12, **12,** 31, **31,** 42, 43
Portuguese man o' war, **12**
Prawn, 35
Pufferfish, 12, **12,** 31, **31,** 42, **42**
Rabbitfish, 59
Rain of fishes, 50
Ray, 17, 23, 42, 59
    Electric ray, 38, **38**
    Manta ray, 39, **39,** 42, **42**
    Sting ray, 21, **21,** 38
    Thornback ray, 28, **28**
Red mullet, **12**
Red tide, 11
Remora, 40, **40**
Reptile, 8
River fish, 13, **13,** 18
Roach, **13,** 49
Roloffia, **36**
Rosy barb, 49
Royal gramma, **37**
Sailfin molly, **36**
Sailfish, 15, **15,** 49
Salmon, **13,** 49, 59
    Egg, 29
    Quinnat salmon, 49
Sandhopper, 17
Sand smelt, 59
Sardine, **24,** 31
    See also Pilchard
Sargasso Sea, 21, 24, 32, 51
Sargassum fish, 21, **21**
Sargassum weed, 21
Sawfish, 31, **31**
Scale, 31, 51
Scorpionfish, 42, **43,** 49, 59
Sea,
    Three types, 12
Sea anemone, 8, **9, 12, 37,** 40–41, **41**
Sea dragon, 20, **20**
Sea fish, 12, **12,** 18, 22
Sea hare, 49
Seahorse, 14–15, **15,** 28, **28,** 59
Sea perch, **12**
Sea serpent, 48
Sea urchin, **9, 12,** 15
Seaweed, 12, **12,** 20–21, 24
Seine net, 44, **44**
Shallow sea fish, 12, **12**
Shark, 8, **12,** 20–24, 49, 59
    Basking shark, 17, **17, 24,** 25, 49
    Blue shark, 49
    Carpet shark, 20, **20**
    Commensalism, 40–41
    Great white shark, 49, 50
    Hammerhead shark, 42, **42**
    Naked gills, 17
    Skin, 31, **31**
    Whale shark, 25
Shrimp, 13
Shrimpfish, 15, **15**
Skate, **12,** 42, 59
Smith, Prof. J.B.L., 43

Smolt, 33, **33**
Soldier fish, 59
Sole, 49
Sperm whale, 48, **48**
Spine, 38, 42
Sprat, 31, 53
Squid, **9,** 48, **48**
Squirrel fish, 59
Starfish, 8, **12**
Stickleback, 25, 26–27, **26–27,** 49, 59
Sting, 21
Stonefish, 20, **20,** 38, **38,** 49
Stone loach, **13**
Sturgeon, 49, 59
Sunda Trench, 50
Surgeon fish, 12, **12**
Swim bladder, 22, **22,** 39, 50, 51
Swordfish, 49–50
Tarpon, 31, 49, 59
Tench, 49
Tetras, 49
Tilapia fish, 27, **27,** 29, **29**
Toad, 8
Torpedo, 38, **38**
Toxic waste, 47
Toxin, 47
Trawl, 34
Triggerfish, 19, **19, 37,** 49
    Queen triggerfish, **37**
Tropical fish, 36–37
Trout, 13, 18, **18,** 49, 59
    Egg, 29
Trumpet fish, 59
Trunkfish, 14–15, **15,** 19, **19,** 31, **31,** 59
Tuna, 12, **12,** 22, 24–25, 47–49, **48,** 53
Turbot, 49
Turkeyfish, 49
Vertebrate, 8
Vinciguerria, 35, **35**
Water flea, 13
Weever, 38, **38**
Whale, 48, **48**
Whale shark, 49, 50
Wobbegong, 20, **20**
Worm, 8, 13
    Marine worm, **9**
Wreckfish, 41, **41**
Xenacanthus, 8, **8**
Zebra fish, 18, **18**

Metric Conversion Table		
1 in.	=	25 millimetres
3 ins.	=	76 millimetres
6 ins.	=	152 millimetres
9 ins.	=	229 millimetres
1 ft.	=	305 millimetres
1 yd.	=	914 millimetres
50 ft.	=	15 metres
100 ft.	=	30 metres